Living
for a
Lifetime

a collection of Life inspired by the lives of others

by Robert H. Steffen

Copyright © 2012 by Robert H. Steffen

Living for a Lifetime

All rights reserved.
Printed in the United States of America.

Living for a Lifetime

Let's be clear right up front.

This is not another "How To" book.
There are countless numbers of those
written by an untold number of authors.
I'm more interested in a "Why For" book,
because until you have a "Why" - and know why,
a library of "How To"s will continue
to gather dust in your Life.
You will find what you are looking for
between these pages, so if I were you,
I would look for something that will shift
your Life in a positive direction!
Finally, my hope is not that you
will get something out of it,
but that it will get something
 amazing out of you...

~Robert H. Steffen

Why do I write ?

OK, here we go.

I've spent several weeks now delaying this,
But it's time you knew the truth; I owe you that much.
Not that long ago, I received a few letters from
someone who questioned why I wrote what I did.
So I went on a mission over the next few nights.
I went through ALL of my posted writings and copied
every comment that anyone had ever left me that spoke of
what a difference I had made because of something I said.
Page... after page... after page...
The one thing that kept echoing in my head was:
"How can I not write ?!!???"
That's the tougher question.
How can I not reach out to someone who needs a hand ?
How can I not share with another who is starving ?
How can I not give to someone who is desperate ?
How can I not touch someone who is within reach ?
You will never know nor even suspect how much
what others have said has done for me.
Not long ago I watched the movie "Pay it Forward".
I have much to say about that movie... another time.
But at one point a lady was about to jump off of a bridge.
What intrigued me was that she didn't look the "type"
of person that would have any real worries -
let alone take her own life. So much for appearances.
Now here comes a strung out druggie who can't seem
to get a leg up in Life and stand on it - not much going
for him at all. He sees her, and tries to talk her down
off the edge of the railing.

She tries telling him it's not his problem, that she's not worth it.
And what he says to her at the end is: "Save MY Life"

I want that to really sink in.
And while you're really getting the depth of that,
I'll tell you something that you already know -
and something that you don't.

I believe that you and I have the power
and capability to make a positive impact
in the lives of those around us.

For those who really DO know this, you also know that
rarely are we aware of it, and seldom will we ever
know it happened ! AND in many cases we're not
even directly involved ! Yet because of our words, our
deeds, our actions - YOU were the catalyst for change;
YOU were the hand that kept me from falling.

Yes, I said "me".
And this is probably the only and last time I will say this.
I've been on that rail; I've been the one who wasn't "worth it".
And it's because of those many Unknowns who have said
"Save MY Life" that have caused me to realize that there is
a greater purpose - and by extending their hand to grab mine,
we've pulled each other to safety.

Why do I write ?
Because of you,

and because of you, I can.

What others are saying...

Awesome, Truly awesome!!!!
Not much more can be said....
you are amazing. You have a gift with words.....
~Lisa Marie

Wow, it is like someone reached into my head
and picked out all of my thoughts and emotions.
I have always wanted to write them down...
and I see now someone has beat me to the bunch.
But at this time, the lowest point in my life,
I find comfort in these words.
knowing that I am not alone in the crazy battle of life.
We all find that even the smallest gesture goes along way.
~Kell

You are truly an amazing person and incredibly
gifted at expressing how life is meant to be lived..
it is something I have been working on for quite a while
and it is truly a miracle that I stumbled upon your site.

It is so great to know that other people think just like me,
and the way you write things fits so perfectly with what
I have been trying so desperately to think and say.

I am so inspired and motivated from your writings to go out and live the life I was intended to. more than I ever have been from my parents. more than I have been from my friends. more than I have been from church.

what you have done here IS making a huge difference, one reader at a time. just touching the life of one person like you have in the past few minutes must be the most rewarding feeling in the world. That something you have said and felt has positively changed someone, and all the other people that that person knows.. what an amazing thing. Thank you so much for the person that you are and for spending the countless hours writing down these ideas (I guess you could call them..) I'm so glad to know that there are others out there like you. I'm so thankful to know that others are trying, actually trying, to make this world a better place. one step at a time, one blog at a time, one affected life at a time. whatever it might be, I can rest assured knowing that there is good in the world.

thanks so much for being who you are and holding nothing back. thank you for being so real. I hope we can connect via email, facebook, myspace, or whatever means of communication are good for you.

I'm so stoked to finally know you, even though I don't really know you! Thank you so much man, You know what is up :) I have only read about 1/6 of your writings and the word excited does not begin to describe how... well... excited I am to continue reading :) Thank you so much my friend, God bless you and your ministry you have started.

~Chris

I really enjoy reading your website.
It is very thought-provoking, and everything is so well stated.
You are very insightful, and a wonderful writer. I loved reading
"The Dance". (one of my all time favorite songs) I think we all
have moments in time we would like to go back and change,
but yet if we had, there are so many wonderful things we would
have missed out on because the outcome would have changed.
"I'm glad I didn't know the way it all would end" because I
wouldn't have had my two beautiful children. :) I wouldn't go
back and change that for anything. Life is a journey and
along that journey we experience many things, and we need
to learn to appreciate the good times in our lives because life
can be bittersweet. I have never been so happy as I am now,
so am glad the events in my life played out the way they did
to lead me to where I am today. Keep up all your great work.
You are an inspiration. :)
~Susan W.

I just couldn't leave your website before letting you
know that I really enjoyed what you offer to your readers...
~Julie C.

You can certainly see your expertise in the work you write.
The world hopes for more passionate writers like you who are not
afraid to say how they believe. Always follow your heart.
~Marek K.

You certainly deserve a round of applause for your work
and more specifically, your writing in general.
Very high quality material
~Karen S.

Great stuff from you, man. I've read your stuff before and you're just too awesome. I love what you've got here, love what you're saying and the way you say it. You make it entertaining and you still manage to keep it smart. I can't wait to read more from you.
~Mary K.

My sister in law posted your website on Facebook and everything she posts really means something to her so I checked it out and I am glad I did. You have so many powerful stories to tell. I am overjoyed by the amount of information each story tell me. They make me think, they make me grow, they make me realize what a beautiful life I already have.
Thank you from the bottom of my heart.
~Bobbi

WOW…..your words have touched me in a way I can not explain….. I like the page thank you for words of wisdom
~Donna

I'm a huge fan already, man. You've done a brilliant job making sure that people understand where you're coming from. And let me tell you, I get it. Great stuff and I can't wait to read More of your work. What you've got to say is important and needs to be read.
~Stephan C.

11 out of 140,342 comments
as of 11-06-2012

Table of Contents:

Why Do I Write?	p.4
What Others Are Saying	p.6
Table of Contents	p.10
Almost	p.14
Always A Reason	p.15
A Moment Like This	p.20
And To Think I Almost Missed It	p.22
Are You Just Killing Time	p.24
Are You Still Waiting...?	p.26
A Wealthy Soul	p.29
Because That's What There is To Do	p.31
Because You're Worth It	p.35
Between You and the Finish Line	p.38
Birds of a Feather	p.42
Being A Part In Changing the World	p.43
Choice More Than Chance	p.44
Choose Your Words Carefully	p.48
Christmas: What Does It Mean...	p.51
COMMUNICATION	p.53
Distractions	p.65
Doing What You Like	p.70
Do You Have $3 To Spare?	p.72
Do You Know How To Fly?	p.74
Do You Want To Be Friends?	p.75
Feeding The Mind	p.79
For Kids and Those Who Care	p.81
For Our Soldiers	p.84

Giving Me My Dream	p.87
GO!	p.92
What If You Gave Your All?	p.94
Gone In 30 Seconds... 30 Years...	p.100
Goodbye	p.103
Live Happily Ever After	p.105
Happy New Year	p.110
Healthcare and our own Health Care	p.113
Hitting The Wall...	p.117
How Do You Want To Feel?	p.119
How Much Do You Want?	p.123
How To Save A Life	p.127
How To Solve Your Problems	p.129
If Only Life Were a Rehearsal	p.132
If People Were More Like Dogs	p.135
If Tomorrow Never Comes	p.137
If You Can't Say Something Nice	p.141
If You Had One Shot	p.143
I Like The Way It Hurts	p.147
I Miss You	p.151
In Another's Shoes	p.153
Independence Day	p.155
Interpretation	p.156
I See Great People	p.158
I Shall Pass This Way But Once	p.162
Is It Really That Bad?	p.165
Is THAT How You Took That?!??	p.168
It Feels Good To Give	p.171

It's Not About The Singing	p.173
Just When You Think	p.176
Let Me Hear Your Song	p.180
Memories In The Making	p.183
Moments Like These	p.187
My Hero For The Day	p.189
No More Excuses!	p.192
Nothing To Lose...	p.195
Now Is A Lucky Time For You -	p.197
Now Is The Time To Break The Chains	p.199
Out Of Sight (Out Of Mind)	p.203
Saving It For The Trip Back	p.207
Scraps of Paper	p.212
Sometimes You Hear Back	p.214
Sticks and Stones May Break My Bones	p.216
Take A Few Minutes	p.218
Take The Chance While...	p.219
The Dance	p.221
The Earth Was Always Round	p.224
The Nail...	p.226
This Will Hurt Me More Than You	p.228
To My Son	p.230
What Are You Hoping Will Save You?	p.231
What Children Can Teach Us	p.234
At The End Of Your Rope	p.236
What Mom Really Said	p.238
What Song Takes You Back?	p.240
What Would You Ask For?	p.243

What Would You Write?	p.245
What You Look For Will Determine...	p.248
When We Give	p.250
Who You Are To Me	p.253
Who You Think You Don't Need To Tell	p.256
Why?	p.259
Why Throw Away Treasure?	p.261
Will You Give Your Life or Live Your Life?	p.264
Would You Change A Thing?	p.269
Would You Have Stopped?	p.271
You And I Are Living Together	p.280
You And I Need Bigger Problems	p.282
You Don't Know What You Don't Know	p.284
Your Life Is An Occasion	p.291
You Will Soon Witness A Miracle	p.293
The Homeless	p.295
Sometimes it Takes A Tragedy	p.299
What Lead You Here?	p.301
~ The End ~ of...?	p.305

Almost

I heard a commercial the other day that talked about
how several people almost gave a man this or that...
and because of it, he almost made it through the night alive.
The point of the commercial was this: Don't "almost" give.
So I took a look at how this applies to my own life. Like so
many things, I was moved by how much I "almost" do.
(Giving is a form of doing - I took it to the next level)
I thought about the friends I've almost kept in contact with,
the family I've almost stayed in touch with,
the son I almost spent enough time with today.
I almost sent out Christmas cards this year... last year... the year before...
Just last week I almost gave money to a bell ringer.
There was a car alongside the road the other day,
and I almost stopped to help.
I almost wrote you a letter...
So many things almost done, and here we are as a result.
Ah, and you thought it was the things in Life that
you had done that got you to your present day life.

Consider just as much those things that you almost did...
You are where you are **and where you aren't** because of them.

You see, I almost finished writing this at Christmas time,
and it almost made a tremendous impact in your Life.
Matter-of-fact, for 5 months now
this has almost meant something to some of you,
and so many more who I may never see or hear from again.
But do you know who it almost made the MOST impact on ?
Me.

> *Stop "Almost" living in your Life...*

Always A Reason

I'm sitting here in a parking lot in my Jeep feeling the breeze
through the open window, and I'm not going to go home until
I finish this. For so many years now I've held a belief that
people come into our lives for a reason - AND sometimes
we know what that reason is, and sometimes we don't.
Chuckle... Do we ever really know ?
And just when we think we know the reason
- Life shifts and we need to think of another reason !
So I guess part two of my belief is that most of the time
we really don't know the reason; and as long as we
come up with a reason that satisfies us, we are content.
I ran across this today and it was the final factor
in finally letting out something I've been
withholding for quite a while:
" ~ Some people come into our lives,
     leave footprints on our heart
     and we are never the same ~ "
I've always wanted to be one of those people.
There have been many a print left on my heart and soul
- people that have made a profound difference in my Life.
And it is my greatest desire and passion to have that
impact in the lives of others. Now is the tricky part.
Do you notice it says "leave footprints on our heart".
What that picture portrays to me is that of footprints;
an impression in one's Life...
and then those prints fade away into the sunset.
So that image brings me to this,
which was emailed to me the other day.
(coincidence or something else ?)

Let it Go by Bishop T.D. Jakes

"There are people who can walk away from you.

And hear me when I tell you this!

When people can walk away from you: let them walk.

I don't want you to try to talk another person

into staying with you, loving you,

calling you, caring about you,

coming to see you, staying attached to you.

I mean hang up the phone.

When people can walk away from you let them walk.

Your destiny is never tied to anybody that left.

People leave you because they are not joined to you.

And if they are not joined to you, you can't make them stay.

Let them go.

And it doesn't mean that they are a bad person

it just means that their part in the story is over.

And you've got to know when people's part in your story

is over so that you don't keep trying to raise the dead.

You've got to know when it's dead.

You've got to know when it's over.

Let me tell you something. I've got the gift of good-bye.

I believe in good-bye.

It's not that I'm hateful, it's that I'm faithful, and I know

whatever God means for me to have He'll give it to me.

And if it takes too much sweat I don't need it.

Stop begging people to stay. Let them go!!

If you are holding on to something that doesn't belong to

you and was never intended for your life, then you need to...

LET IT GO!!!

If you are holding on to past hurts and pains .

LET IT GO!!!

If someone can't treat you right, love you back, and see your worth...

LET IT GO!!!

If someone has angered you ...

LET IT GO!!!

If you are holding on to some thoughts of evil and revenge...

LET IT GO!!!

If you are involved in a wrong relationship or addiction...

LET IT GO!!!

If you are holding on to a job that

no longer meets your needs or talents .

LET IT GO!!!

If you have a bad attitude...

LET IT GO!!!

If you keep judging others to make yourself feel better...

LET IT GO!!!

If you are struggling with the healing of a broken relationship...

LET IT GO!!!

If you keep trying to help someone

who won't try to help themselves...

LET IT GO!!!

If you're feeling depressed and stressed ...

LET IT GO!!!

Let the past be the past. Forget the former things.

LET IT GO!!! "

OK, are you back ? I am.

What I'm trying to say is that for a long time

I've felt very guilty about not being really "connected".

Come on, you that know me well can get this.

I'm aloof, keep to myself & a loner for the most part.

Yet, rather than try to keep fighting this,

I'm beginning to learn that it's OK.

Just because people can make a difference in my Life

doesn't mean I have to cling to them,

just as if I happen to make a difference in the Life of another

do I need to feel compelled to stay close or cling to them.

OK, so read this if I've lost you a bit.

(below author unknown :( )

"People come into your life for a reason, a season, or a lifetime.

When you figure out which it is, you know exactly what to do.

When someone is in your life for a REASON, it is usually

to meet a need you have expressed outwardly or inwardly.

They have come to assist you through a difficulty,

to provide you with guidance and support,

to aid you physically, emotionally, or spiritually.

They may seem like a godsend, and they are.

They are there for the reason you need them to be.

Then, without any wrong doing on your part

or at an inconvenient time, this person will say or do

something to bring the relationship to an end.

Sometimes they die. Sometimes they walk away.

Sometimes they act up or out and force you to take a stand.

What we must realize is that our need has been met,

our desire fulfilled; their work is done.

The prayer you sent up has been answered and it is now time

to move on. When people come into your life for a SEASON,

it is because your turn has come to share, grow, or learn.

They may bring you an experience of peace or make you laugh.

They may teach you something you have never done.

They usually give you an unbelievable amount of joy.

Believe it! It is real! But, only for a season. "

Now, if you're feeling like asking me

or anyone else which you are to them,

or what you may be to them - don't. Just. Don't.

The only way you'll ever know if someone is to be in your

life forever is at the end of your life - and they are still there.

The people that fall out of touch - they are blessings either
of a Season or for a Reason. Key word = blessing.
And what do you do with a blessing ? Be thankful !!! Sheesh.
At times I've been sad that people have drifted out of my life.
But I've been blessed by them, so that is what I hold onto.
And you know, if I've made any of you smile or laugh;
comforted you in sorrow or grief...
Maybe that was my reason for being in your Life;
perhaps this is our Season of experience.
Who knows. I know I'll never really know.
But... I have an opinion ;)
It seems to me that every person who would be a
part of our lives - especially for our Lifetime
would start out as a Reason.
So with that in mind, I think it's pretty awesome
that of all the billions of people in this world,
and of all the millions of things to read -
YOU are reading this from ME.

And guess what ? I have another opinion. ...
I think there's a reason you're reading this
just as I think there's a reason I am writing it
at this exact hour on this particular day.

And I may never know what it is...

A Moment Like This

Not too long ago I was listening to a song I've heard many
many times before. It wasn't a song I particularly like, but
on this day I really heard it. What stood out for me was
this part of the chorus: *"...a moment like this;*
Some people wait a lifetime - For a moment like this "
Many things came to mind, namely that I couldn't
think of a moment that I had NOT waited a lifetime for.
That's what our life is comprised of: moments!
So I thought about how much we wait for these "moments".
Do you realize that there is a good chance that the very
"moment" that we wait and wait and wait for is happening
somewhere else in the world at this very moment ?
What I would also dare to mention is that this "moment"
is happening because someone else did not wait for it
to happen, but rather went after it and made it happen.
"SOME people wait a lifetime for a moment like this"
Yes, some people do - while other people are living them.
By now at least one of us has realized that I am going
in an entirely different direction than I had originally planned.
But do you realize that we spend far too much time waiting ?
We wait for the right timing
We wait for the right moment
We wait for the right opportunity.
What if what we wait for never arrives ?
I'm reminded of a story I heard a long time ago,
and I wonder if I haven't told you this already.

A man was going through his wife's dresser while his
Brother sat nearby. As he went through, he mentioned
things about several pieces that he came across.

At one point he came across a beautiful outfit - I think
it may have been some fancy lingerie from New York.
You can tell it's bringing back memories, and he tells
his brother that he'd never seen her in it yet -
that she'd been saving it for a special occasion.
"Well, it looks like this is it..." he told his brother.
Tears filled his eyes as he said this, and suddenly
he turned to his brother, exclaiming;
 "Never save anything for a 'special occasion' "
and he placed the outfit with the rest
of the clothes for her funeral...

Listen,
you and I both have something
that we're waiting for just the right time,
moment, or opportunity to make happen.
If you don't have any - let me give you a few of mine !
But I've got to tell you,
the day will come when it really will be too late.

**Let your "special occasion"
be every breathe you take;
every new day you awaken
and are blessed to be alive.**

And To Think I Almost Missed It

My favorite stories are about people
helping others in need, and not long ago
I saw hundreds of people doing just that.
In this case it was an entire community reaching
out to a boy (about my son's age) and his family.

For those who attended the Team Tyler fundraiser,
you saw what I saw; people from all around giving
of their time, energy, resources, love, and support.
You saw not only those who were affected by Tyler
and the Batten Disease that he battles, but also the
effect that the family has had on those around them.
The kind of effect that moves both friend and
stranger alike to not only make the event a success;
but to bring with each day continued support,
love, and encouragement long after the tables
are folded up and the chairs put away.

So let me ask you something, and I hope you'll be honest;
Who do you know that could use some kind of help ?
Now who do you **not** know who could also use help ??
Here's why I ask.

I never knew who Tyler Allman was before that Saturday,
and it was only through a friend of mine that I found out.
I didn't have much to give, but I gave all I had gratefully.

And though I am only one person,
one at a time we became hundreds.

My experience in having been there
left me much the richer in encouragement,
inspiration, and appreciation for people and
their capacity to be united in love & compassion.

You just can't put a price on that...
And to think I almost missed it –
just because I didn't know them.
Don't miss out on the opportunity to help another -
you may never know what you're missing,
nor what an incredible difference you can make.

Are You Just Killing Time?

By the time you had your 1st Birthday
(Happy belated Birthday !) the earth spun around
the sun and you passed the 31,536,000 second mark.
Over an average lifetime, that's 2,112,912,000 seconds !!!
Just think about it - TWO BILLION seconds.
You've got all kinds of time !
35,215,200 minutes to do whatever you want.
586,920 hours to do with what you will.
24,455 days to just... do whatever
3,493 weeks to live the dream 804 months - Que Sera Sera !
67 years to... The End. Curtains close. Whoa...

How did we get to such a small number ?
The average person in this world lives
to ride this merry Go Round 67 times.
Now, we probably won't be doing a whole lot of
individual thinking & planning for at least 15 years.
Parents & politics (schooling) will be doing that for us.
So, really, we're down to 52 years.
Ah, but "we" - WE, as in You and Me;
heck, if you're reading this I'd be amazed if you
aren't at LEAST 20; surprised if you are under 30.
Now, I am using a calculator to figure all of this -
which means we can safely say that we're now
down to 37 spins on the Weeeeeorld.
That's... not a lot of candles.

A few weeks ago (about 1209600 seconds ago)
I heard someone say typically after work they
just like to go home and "Kill time" by
watching T.V. until it's time for dinner.
And.... I just couldn't...
I could not get my mind into a mode where I
could just allow time to simply pass by without Life.

Killing time.
That to me is something that might be said
of someone on death row; just killing time:
waiting for time to pass before The End.

How can anyone live and breathe on the
same planet I am and simply... kill time?
With only 37 more free dinners at IHOP!

What is it we're focusing on and how blind are we
that killing time is just something "normal" we do?
What are we listening to that we don't hear
the needs of others... and ourselves?

Don't be casual about the moments you have left;
don't waste your Life by merely "killing time".
Turn off the music, stop looking in the mirror;

Look... Listen... now L I V E !

Are You Still Waiting
For That Second Chance?

Earlier this afternoon I heard these words out of the radio:
"Spend all your time waiting for that second chance..."
I had to grab a pen & paper and write it down before I forgot.
There was too much that it triggered to let it go.

Do you know what "all your time" is ? That's your Life.
Do you know what "waiting" is?
It's that time you spend not taking action.
Do you know what a "second chance" is?
It's usually that thing you let fear take away
- or allowed failure to run off with the first time.

Many of us spend a great deal of our lives allowing
fear and failure to take away what which we desire.
We imagine so often how those missed opportunities
might have turned out differently if only...
Well if only things had been different.
And of course we can say that because they remain just that;
missed opportunities; that second chance we never got.
It's almost... as if a second chance was expected.

Not long ago I was given an all too familiar
reminder that this Life of ours - the one
we're living moment to moment,
was not a dress rehearsal.
It's the real deal.

The lights have been on, the cameras rolling;
and we've been living out the script of our truths.

I found it a bit ironic when I received that message,
because I'm the one always "reminding" others
that there is no dress rehearsal in this Life -
and yet the face that looks back in the mirror
every morning is the one who continues
to live as if this is just a practice run.
Trust me, and you may have grown wise to this,
but there's a reason I'm my most avid reader.
I point the finger at you,
and 3 more point back to me.
And yes, I am my harshest critic –
just like you are to you!

Ah, but enough about me –
back to that second chance.

When you think about it (or when you don't)
the odds of scenarios and circumstances occurring
the same way twice are staggeringly against you.
So this second chance we're hoping for...
Good luck with that.

Here's what you should consider and focus on:
Your next chance - because that IS the first chance.
Always.

ALWAYS.

What an amazing realization to grasp !

No more waiting around for a second chance at anything,
because we have before us the opportunity to create
a first chance at any given moment of any given day
to anything we set our hearts and minds to.

We always have,
and we have been - always.

To say that is good to know
would be an understatement.

Now, stop practicing your lines
and preparing to be "perfect".

You're on.

A Wealthy Soul

The other day as I was driving the song "Travelin' Man"
by Bob Seger came on the radio.
My sister was a Bob Seger fan when I was a kid,
and I never really got "into" her kind of music.
So I'm listening, because now it's reminding me of her,
and at the same time - reminding me of home.

"Leavin my home, leavin my friends,
Runnin when things get too crazy..."

I nod to myself - how true how true;
that's how I ended up in the Northwest !
And then I heard this:

"Sometimes at night, I see their faces,
I feel the traces they left on my soul.
Those are the memories
that made me a wealthy soul."

So much still comes to mind & tugs at my heart;
I'm pulled back to sitting at a piano at the house
of my very first girlfriend & we're both playing
(some simple tune that goes da da da... da da da da da da da
da da da da da da da da da da da da da da da da da da da)
((Come on - you know the one !))

The sweet memory of kissing my best friend's cousin on the
beach in Florida over Christmas break - my first REAL kiss ;)
Seeing my son born; realizing what an incredible love
I have helped bring into the world...

Falling hopelessly in love for the first time.
A 'thank you' card that says
"Rob, I appreciate you"
love, Chris.

My Mom & Dad holding their grandson for the first time...
I was so very very proud. ...

And then I thought about something I read
not long ago sent to me by a friend.
If you only knew
how much your encouragement
and your belief in me has meant.
The little things you've said -
ripples that continue to make their way
back & forth across the lake of my heart.

Yes, these...
and countless more
past and yet to be:

these are the memories
that make me a wealthy soul...

Because That's What There is To Do

It's midnight, Sunday
- I'm sitting in my Jeep at a rest stop.
Some things can't wait.
Ever since last night a line has been repeating itself
over and over in my head.

"There are bigger things at work here..."

It's a line (or close to it) from one of the Spider Man movies.
Spider Man is battling with an enemy
who not long ago was his best friend.
Not sure the whole story - only that other enemies
are wreaking havoc on the general public
and his girlfriend's life is in jeopardy.
His friend could only focus on what he thought Spider Man
had done, which was kill his father (a.k.a. the Green Goblin).
He didn't see the bigger picture; that many people
- including those he cared about, were in danger.
In his world, all he could see was that he had been wronged,
and he wanted revenge; to get back...
Eventually he saw beyond his own blind ambitions
and helped Spider Man fight and defeat the enemy
- giving his very Life for the greater cause.

You and I -
We have... so many battles.

Another month further behind
on our bills, with no end in sight.
A daughter out of control,
defiant and disrespectful
- her mother crying herself
to sleep at night wondering
what she did wrong.
What seemed like a promotion
in an aspiring company ends in
unemployment as the company
folds and closes its doors.

The phone call that brings the news
that the treatment didn't take and now
they need to start chemotherapy...
She hangs up the phone, fighting back the tears.
Her daughter is in the living room playing the piano, unaware.
Down the hall in his room her teenage son chats online.
Her husband is on his way home from work, oblivious -
just another day for him, wondering what's for dinner.
Suddenly her son's messy room doesn't seem to bother her.
Her daughter's "C" in math... well it could be worse.
So her husband is working late again for the overtime
- she feels grateful rather than the usual resentment.
The roast beef is almost done,
she quickly makes a salad while the potatoes cool.
At some point before the night is through,
the rest of the family will know about the cancer
and come together in support
- Because that's what there is to do.

Because that's what there is to do.

What do you do when you get knocked down ?
How do you handle Life's disappointments,
setbacks, challenges, and even betrayals ?
When you're on your knees with
the wind sucked out of you,
what do you do ?
Where do you go ?
What do you blame... or who ?
How long do you stay there?
...or are you still there even now ?
Because that's what
there is to do..

It is not because I lack compassion
that I say what I am about to say,
but rather because there are bigger things
at work here - and I cannot allow my
fear of what you may think of me
prevent me from saying it.

We can wish things were different,
and we all too often wallow in our pain,
our misery, our anger, pity, and shame.
Meanwhile, time marches on, the world turns
- and Life moves on without us.

If you want to keep up –
if you want to conquer,
you've got to get up
and put one foot in
front of the other
and move.

Nothing happens until you make it happen,
and until you step up, look in the mirror
and realize that YOU ultimately decide and
determine your fate and place in this World
- you will always stumble and fall further
from the Life you wish you had.

You need to find what it is that is Bigger... than you.
Your family needs you to, your friends need you to.
Your community and country needs you to,
and if you can truly embrace what I do
- the World needs you to.

But let's start with you first,
because you really need you to first.

That's why I'm sitting at a rest stop
writing you, at 2am

- because that's what there was to do
        and that's where I needed to begin.

Because You're Worth It

The other day I was talking with a
client who has read several of my
writings, and he shared with me
something which he believed
about people and their health.

In short: If a person doesn't really care about themselves,
they aren't going to take good care of themselves.
Though recently I have focused my time and energy
into the more tangible areas of health, none of that
will make a difference to those who do not hold
a healthy image of themselves to begin with.
I mean really - if I don't care whether or not
I'm going to die in 10 years, why bother ?
If there is nothing in my Life worth living for,
why take care of it or treat it with respect?
You won't hear many people say this out loud,
nor will most people even say it to themselves.
Many won't even think it... But look around.
Read the news. Look at the statistics.
A LOT of people are in bad shape !
And no matter what you and I try to share with them
that would make their life better - they will not embrace it;
for they do not and will not accept & embrace themselves.

Here's what I know that they don't,
and I know this from experience.
Let me be that small voice that
they may not be hearing;
because you're worth it. You are.

I heard it said well 20 years ago by a fellow named Zig Ziglar.

He had said: "If you had a million dollar racehorse,

would you keep it up all night letting it eat junk food,

smoke cigarettes, drink booze, and watch TV?"

Of course you wouldn't!

You'd find him the best veterinarian and feed

him the most nutritious and healthiest food.

You'd provide him the best trainer and

make sure he got plenty of exercise.

You would go out of your way to make

sure that million dollar racehorse was

treated like a million dollar racehorse!

But what about that billion dollar body...

and that priceless mind?

Well, How are you treating it, my Friend?

I just can't picture a million dollar racehorse eating

a microwaved pizza with a 6 pack of beer, while smoking a

cigarette & watching some brain numbing reality TV show.

Except... maybe Mr. Ed. (And I lied - I CAN picture it!) Ugh...

There are only 2 reasons:

1) They don't know any better

2) They don't care enough to do better

Bottom line is - whether you realize it or not -

your physical health IS connected to your mental health.

How you think and feel about yourself

will be reflected by how you treat yourself.

* If you know something is good for you,

   why wouldn't you include it in your life?

Really take a look at whatever answer you have for this.

Seriously.
I'm worth fresh green beans
instead of frozen or canned.
I'm worth sliced apples
instead of processed & sugar filled Apple Jacks.
I'm worth breathing fresh air into my lungs
without carcinogens & chemicals.
I'm worth knowing what is harming my body
and what I can do to counteract it.
I'm worth at least a half hour of exercise a day
to boost the cardiovascular.
I'm worth learning the truth
instead of what outside influences want me to believe.
I'm worth the time and effort it takes to learn
what IS good for me instead of going after
the convenient, familiar, and popular.

My Mom used to (and probably still does!) have a saying.
      "You know better than that!"
This usually came right after my brother or I did something
that was probably not the brightest idea or we did
something without really thinking about it, OR
simply because we wanted to do it anyway.
You know how kids are.

You and I are adults.
I can't say that you know better than that - because
I know what the popular and common belief systems are.
All I can do is share what I've found because I care about YOU –
and hope YOU care about yourself enough to want to know better.

And don't make me bring my Mom in here...

Between You and the Finish Line

I watched a young football player crawl on his hands and feet
(NOT knees) 100 yards – with a 160lb kid on his back.
And he did it blindfolded - believing all the while that
he could only go and was only going 30 yards.
(note: you MUST see the movie "Facing the Giants")

So what is it that you carry;
what burdens or baggage do you have
that keeps you from going the distance ?
Yep – you better believe I'm jumping in
with both feet on this one, so either run
with me or sit on the sidelines and hope
 someone else calls you in the game!

As I'm sitting here I cannot think of
a single person who does not have at
least one thing that is holding them
back in some way in their Life.
So can we just assume that this may just apply
to you as well as it does to me and continue ?
I feel like I should throw that out there early
so that we're all on an even playing field.
And for those of you sitting on the fence
about this, just humor me.
We'll both feel better about it later.
Good.

So, If I took away some of your burdens,
do you think you could go further in
whatever endeavors you chose to pursue?
What if I removed some of the baggage
in your Life that has constantly held you
back from going after something
that you've really – really wanted.

There's a good chance you'd dig in your
heels and give it your best shot, huh?
Come on – be honest :)
Don't worry, I'm not going to ask you
to get rid of your "baggage".
Many people hold onto that so tight
you'd think it was going to earn
them a medal of honor!
So keep it –
I'm sure it makes for great conversation.

Now, back to this great endeavor of yours.
Maybe if I brought it nearer. Perhaps if it was
just a bit closer to you - within a more reasonable
distance, now THAT would surely help, right ?!?

Let me throw something out there
that may twist some popular thinking.
Take your eyes off the goal.
And remember – I'm only talking to those of you
who cannot move forward another foot, another inch;
and your destination – your goal – is simply beyond reach.
Stop looking at the goal.

I say this because when I'm looking down the field,
there's the goal — waaaaaaaaaaaay down there -
and then I see all the grass in between.
I see all the grass, the markings;
all the "stuff" that isn't the goal.
All the stuff that isn't the goal.
Showing me how far I have to go.
Because here's what I've observed:

You're going to get going and before long
distractions will deter your focus, and you'll
become consumed by how far you have to go
and how hard it's getting. And you'll stop at
just about as far as you believed you could go.

Let me throw this example out there.
Back in high school track I was at a meet,
and it was taking place at a rival high school.
Note: I was not the fastest runner on our team.
The track was an inside track — shorter and unfamiliar.
At some point there was a trial run, and long story short
I chose to keep pace with a couple of runners from
the other school. It never dawned on me that
I'd picked their best runners to run with!
All I know was that I kept up with them -
and it took everything I had to do it.

Guess what I found out later in the week?
My time for that run (1/2 mile) was better
than the fastest recorded for our school.
I had broken our school record in the 1/2 mile!

40

Of course, you'll never find it in the history books,
because it was not an actual race – only a trial run.
Why is this story relevant?
Because I was essentially blindfolded.

I didn't see the usual markers to know
that I should've been pacing myself on the
first 2 laps, picking up the pace on the
3rd, then pouring it on the 4th.
I couldn't see the runners on our team
who had always been "faster" than I –
because this time they were behind me.

> I couldn't see the things
> that would usually tell me
> how fast and how far I could go.

Remember that.
If you do not see those things
that would tell you how far you can go
you will go much further than
you believe yourself capable.

You won't spend your time & energy looking
at all of the "stuff" that isn't a part of your goals.
And those things that seem so far away and out of reach
will soon be closer than you think. And as odd as it sounds,
sometimes it takes having a blindfold on to see the goal

Birds of a Feather;

Are They Going The Right Way?!?

"Birds of a feather flock together..."

This may be an age old bit of wisdom
- but what I really want to know is:
Do I know where the flock is headed,
and do I want to go where they're going ?

So my thinking for the day is that
it is more important to be in a "flock"
that is going where you want to go in Life.
I think this whole birds of a feather thing came about
because it's so comfortable and easy to develop
friendships & associations with those who are more like us.
We also tend gather those around us who agree with us.
Notice I didn't say those who support us.
The two are very different;
you can support someone in their decisions
without having to agree with them.
So, as much as it's easy, warm, fuzzy, cozy, etc.
to be in a group of people like me
who will carry me along; I'd rather be pulled
by those headed in the direction I want to go.

Now. Where do YOU want to go?

Being A Part
In Changing the World

It was not that long ago that I was asked
what I wanted to do when I grew up.
"Be a part in changing the World" was my response.

As many of you know – I can't do this.
But I have faith that some of YOU can…
How long does it take to move a mountain ?
Over a lifetime – if only one person is doing it.

So tell me - What if you had 150,000 people to help
you move that mountain ? Rather inspiring, isn't it ?
Makes that daunting task of mountain moving seem
a bit more achievable & realistic. And what if each
of those 150,000 people shared the cause of moving
this mountain with just a couple of their friends?
In no time at all we'd have 450,000 people ready,
willing and able to move the mountain with
very little effort on any one person's part.
That's almost half a million!

Now, even if we never find that "One" person who can
manage to transform the world with their amazing greatness;
we can look back and find that each of us managed to
change the world all by ourselves - one person at a time.

So here's my little secret. 152,264 is the number of page views
I've had as of tonight. That's how many opportunities there
have been to change the world one person at a time.

      And now it's your turn… We could use another hand :)

Choice More Than Chance
Brings You What You Hope For...

Uncertainty repeated
creates a self fulfilling doubt,
which causes further uncertainty.

Speak of those things you desire,
focus on that which can be certain
and set the sails of your heart
to the winds of passion.

Choice

more than chance

brings you what you hope for...

Ever caught yourself saying things like:
> I'm not sure if I can do that
> I don't know if that will work
> I may not finish it on time

Here's the deal.
It's one thing to be unsure of something.
I mean, we all have our doubts at times.
But one of the surest way to magnify that is to
keep repeating it to yourself, and especially to others.
Every time you repeat how you doubt something will work,
or how you're not sure of this or that - you are imbedding
that thought deeper and deeper in your mind as a truth.
And your mind will come up with ingenious ways to
make sure your doubts and uncertainties come true.

And those around you that hear you say it ?
What they now know is that you are not accountable;
that your ability to get something done cannot be relied on,
and that you do not believe in yourself enough to do it.
So they, like you, will begin planning on your inability
rather than rallying behind your ability to get the job done.

This divides efforts and resources, which further
Weakens the possibility of reaching the desired
outcome efficiently and expediently.
And this happens at work, at home; wherever you are.

So let's look at this differently.
I threw out a few fairly basic but common thoughts earlier.
Let's twist them a bit.
> "I'm not sure if I can do that"

Sounds like one more thing I can cross off
of my "I've never done this before" list.
Do you realize that everything from walking to
riding a bike was once on this same list ?
Trust me - most of the things you will do in Life
have been done by other people before.
So, you already know it can be done.
It's just your turn to get it done.
Go get it done.

> "I don't know if that will work"

I heard that's what Henry Ford's engineers said
when he told them he wanted to have a V-8 engine.
Actually, I believe a few of them said it was impossible.

Just because some thing or some solution exists in the realm
of unknown to you does not mean that it does not exist.
It will work, and there is a way.   Find it.

> "I may not finish it on time"

First of all, let's get rid of the whole " I I I me me me"
Let's try "It will be done in time".
That way you're not stuck relying on just you.
Look at your projects through 3D "glasses".
Distraction Delegation Dedication

Distraction is the #1 reason things are not done on time.
Stay focused on the important - do not allow the shinier
seemingly urgent things keep taking you off task.

Delegation is the key to productivity.
There are things that you can do, and do well.
There are things that others can do, and do well.
Delegate the aspects of a given project that do not
require your expertise so that you may devote the
specialized skills that you have to its completion.

If a doctor has 4 hours to perform a heart transplant, I can
guarantee you that he will not be answering phones, writing
invoices, or running around looking for scalpels & swabs.
It's not that he can't - it's that he knows that the best use
of his time is applying his specialized skills before deadline.
Literally, in this case.

Dedication is simply not giving up,
and giving up is a conscious choice.

Do what needs to be done - because that's what there is to do.
There is no letting yourself off the hook if you are dedicated.

Well, I didn't mean to get so much into details here, although
sometimes it helps to have a few tools to keep one on track.
But if I were to choose which one was most important,
I'd say the most important part is the beginning:

~"Uncertainty repeated
creates a self fulfilling doubt,
which causes further uncertainty..."

**"The more you doubt,
the more doubt you create**. ~"

"Speak of those things you desire,
focus on that which can be certain
and set the sails of your heart
to the winds of passion."

Talk about what you want to happen – share the desired result
and the positive expectations you have; let those be
the words both you and others hear and reinforce.

**Choice - more than chance
          brings you what you hope for...**

YOU choose what thoughts that you allow to
simmer and develop into the actions you will take –
and take you - to where you want to be.

You can be certain of that :)

Choose Your Words Carefully -
They Affect Us Far More Than You Know

If a friend of yours, or someone you respected told you
that you looked sick today would you believe them?
If a complete stranger told you that you looked
sick today would you believe them?
If a half a dozen people told you that you
looked sick today would you believe them?

Would you at least wonder that if that many people
told you looked sick today there may be a chance
that you may be coming down with something ?
And as you begin to ponder this possibility, you become
very aware of every sensation in your body.
Every blink, bump and blemish becomes evidence
that there is indeed something wrong with you.

Then begin to ask yourself and others if you look sick.
And it isn't long before you really do begin looking ill,
and your body accepts the reality that
has been created of being sick.

This is not new information.
We've long had cases where perfectly healthy people were
convinced that they weren't healthy and soon developed
symptoms of the illness they were purported to have.
The words said to us by ourselves and others have a
profound and very real effect on us, which is to say
that the words we hear directly affect our very lives.

So here we are in the third month
of the year two thousand and nine.
I think it is safe to say that we are in a crisis.
After all, didn't our very own President - the leader of the
most powerful country on earth tell us this just a month ago?

      "A failure to act, and act now,

      will turn crisis into a catastrophe."

(kudos to his speech writers; I enjoy well crafted phrases)

How long ago did we hear that we were in a recession ?
I think that started several years ago.
And oh sure - many in "power" denied it -
but the seed had been planted, repeated often enough
and finally accepted by us. You know; "We the people".
That "us". So naturally we acted as if there was a recession,
and the evidence came forth to support it; and we all smiled
at ourselves for being responsible and taking action.

And now that we are experiencing such tumultuous
economic times: we are rolling up our sleeves again.
And once again we are creating the very chaos
that we hope to cure. Everywhere I turn I hear
media sources espousing these "tough economic times"
as if there were a reward for it. Their efforts are paying off,
because even at work I am hearing phrases like:
"times are tough"
"in this economy"
"in times like these"
"an economy like this"
"with the economy like it is"
"in these tough economic times"
"with the economy the way it is"

And with every breath; every word uttered,
we reinforce it - and make it so.

I am surely no Pollyanna;
nor an optimist without a sense of reality.
The following might sound political only because many of the
words can be found within the camps of the politically minded.

The salvation we seek in these "troubled times"
will not come from any bailout or "package".
The quick fixes and short term solutions created to appease
a majority of short sighted and impatient individuals
will consistently cause many times more harm
than any amount of temporary healing.
(For those who need a visual example, try
putting out a fire by throwing gasoline on it)

We will create the economy we experience
by the efforts and energies we put into it.
It will not come from a press release.
It will not be handed down from on high.

If you are looking for a green light -
you've got it: GO SUCCEED !!!
Y O U can and will make a contribution
to not only your own life, but to the lives
of those around you by creating it
within the words you speak.

Choose your words carefully - please.

Christmas: What Does It Mean, And What Meaning Do We Give It?

The other day my 9 year old son says to me:
"Dad – I don't really play with Hotwheels anymore.
Is it OK if I pick out some for Adam for Christmas, because
he really likes them." I told him I thought that was a great idea.
And instead of going through and picking out the ones he
didn't want - he went through and chose the ones he thought
Adam would like. Very carefully, he placed them in a Triscuit
box to wrap later. I secretly hoped his friend would not
mind that the toys were not new – still in the box.
Kids play with toys still, not boxes – right?
It seems so much of society is wrapped up in presentation
and looks instead of the content and what is really important.
And… I've got to tell you that this caused me
to look at what I was doing this Christmas.
I didn't like that I was rushing around trying to make sure I
got presents for everyone who I thought was expecting gifts.
Was I really so caught up in the mainstream and media's
definition & presentation of Christmas that I'd lost sight
of what the spirit of the season was about?
Christmas when I was a kid was more about spending time
with family, visiting relatives and being with loved ones.
Sure, there were presents – and it was fun getting them!
But as I got older, the joy shifted to what I could give
instead of what I might be getting all wrapped up with bows.
It's hard to say when obligation and guilt began dictating what
Christmas would look like more than love and a giving spirit.
Perhaps in moving and living far away from family & friends
it was easier to give presents to them rather than presence.

Is this where we are today?

Are we so removed from one another that we would rather
send intangible emails rather than real and genuine cards,
signed, sealed and delivered? Do we drop ship packages
instead of showing up on their doorstep? Are we too busy
buying "stuff", decorating homes and trees, and worrying
about stuffing over potatoes and homemade VS bought
that we aren't spending time sharing our hearts
and showing our Love for one another?
Is the glow of a television more important to have
all eyes glued to it instead of actually doing things like
playing games with each other & interacting with reality?

Seriously, call this a serendipity – but if nothing else I hope
that this economy has caused people to give more of themselves
rather than what their bank account could dictate and afford.
Because there is no greater gift, no treasure of more worth
than taking the time to share heart to heart and face to face;
to both reach within ourselves while reaching out to others.
And if we can't be with the families that we grew up with,
what a beautiful stretch to share it with our brothers
and sisters of this world, both known and unknown.

There was One who gave His best to us… for us.
The very Reason for the Season was given up as a Gift to us
that we might have a better Life and live it more abundantly.

It is my hope that this year, and every day along the way
we share with and show our fellow mankind a kind of love
that gives unconditionally and without expectation the best
of who we are and what we have to offer.
And above all else, Love…

COMMUNICATION:

I Don't Care What You Say - What Do You MEAN ??!!???

How well do you think you know

what it is the people in your World are saying?

Do you know if that's what they meant??

Some time ago I happened to see a commercial from a

popular cell phone company that gave some examples

of how a dropped call can really ruin a conversation.

In one case, a guy calls his girl on the phone,

and the conversation goes like this:

"(M) Hey baby (F) Hey - What's up?

(M) Not much. Just wanted to talk to the most beautiful

    girl in the world, that's all. (F) That's sweet :)

(M) It's true! (F) Yeah, yeah...

(M) It's just nice to know that I'm the only man in your world.

(Call drops - Silence from her end)(pause... pause... pause...)

(M) I am the only man in your world... right ? (F) silence...

(M) Baby ?? (F) silence...

(M) Baby... Is it... is it... Earl ? (F) silence...

(M) Cat got your tongue?? (F) silence...

(M) Earl got your tongue ?!?!! "

So we can probably play out this scenario ourselves.

He gets ticked, probably says a few choice words.

Spends the rest of the day wondering what's wrong,

finally gets fed up with it & goes to a bar that night

looking for this Earl character. Gets in a fight.

And that's it !!! She's not even worth the trouble.
It's OVER, and he is done with her games
and how dare she cheat on him
after all he's done for her !

Oops. Went a little overboard there.
* STOP *
Jot this down:

"Where there is silence,
there is often assumption:
and we tend to fill the void
with answers born of doubt and fear."

* CONTINUE *

I wish I could say that I'm exaggerating with my take on the
'What Happens Next' in the commercial, and you know I am.
BUT I HAVE seen this kind of thing happen -
and I have even had it happen to me!
Not a dropped cell phone call;
but a dropped communication between people.

Do you know what a dropped communication is ?
It's any communication that is not received as delivered;
a communication where the interpretation
is different than the intended meaning.

Given that interpretation happens internally,
there is no way of knowing if something is being
understood correctly or being unknowingly confused.
And Where there is silence, there is usually assumption.

So check this out. I'm at a friend's house and his 4 year old son is about to stick the end of some toy into an electrical outlet. Yikes ! Fortunately, the dad stops him -and tells him not to do it and that he could get electrocuted !!! And finishes it up with a stern "Do you understand?!??" His son nodded sincerely and said "yes". Disaster avoided... Right???
Seriously? SERIOUSLY ?!?!?!?
Understand what? What was he supposed to understand ??
DOES HE EVEN KNOW WHAT THE WORD
"UNDERSTAND" EVEN MEANS ?!?!?

Guess what? As we get older, we know more things
and become familiar with what more words mean.
And while this is all well and good, it also becomes
more dangerous. Because we think we know
what a person means by the things they say.

Let's be real. I'm pretty sure we all think that
we are good communicators, and most people
I know for the most part say what they mean.
Precisely the trap.
You say what you mean, and leave it to
the other person to KNOW what you meant.
And chances are they hear what you're saying
and interpret it to mean what THEY THINK it means.
Here is the "missing" in at 98% of the conversations I hear.
Affirmation of interpretation.
When you ask someone "Do you know what I mean?"
they'll usually say "yes" most of the time, and if they don't
know and ask you to repeat it - you may repeat or explain
it in a different way BUT UNLESS you have them affirm
what they thought you said, you're still just rolling the dice.

Even though you may say something in a different way
and ask if they understood it better that time -
IF the response is "Yes, thank you for clearing that up"
HOW DO YOU KNOW IT'S REALLY CLEARED UP ?!?

I am doing my best to hammer this home
and if it seems redundant, so be it.
I'd rather be redundant than unclear -
because I cannot tell you what being casual and
assumptive in my own communication has cost me.
It's one of the main reasons I have halted all other projects
until this one is finally "out there" in the Universe.
So consider this piece the "Rainbow" after the storm!
The key is in realizing that everything IS interpreted.
Everything. EVERY. THING. Always. A L W A Y S.
And this interpretation is based on what WE know.
So what does our knowing consist of ?
Our past experiences, lessons, understanding, and
everything our brain has gathered up to this point.
But the wild card is this:
It's all OUR knowledge & experience; not the other person's.
Even if you're a twin, and an identical one like myself, you still
don't know what the other knows. You still don't know for sure
what the other person means until they tell you and you tell them.

And finally - we're at a solution.
A simple and easy solution to the biggest cause
of breakdown and chaos between people.
If you are being told anything that might be even
remotely important, repeat back to the person saying it:
1) What you heard
2) What you think it meant

Rinse. Repeat as needed until the words run clear.

I'd love to see you work this into your daily conversations.
If you do this with the intent of creating a better understanding
of what people mean when they say the things they say -
you may be surprised at how often the words they use
do not convey the originally intended message.

Now, do you remember what I told you to jot down earlier?
Did you ?? (If not - why not?)
"Where there is silence,
there is often assumption:
and we tend to fill the void
with answers born of doubt and fear."

Remember the commercial dialogue at the beginning?
This is a whole new can of worms. Just as the words we say
and hear can cause so much confusion, more so can silence.
Because with silence - we have only our own self to sort.
And it is human nature to wonder what might be wrong
when an immediate "this is right" is not present.
We make the silence mean something other than
what it really is: the space between words.
We build stories from the projections of our fears,
doubts, inadequacies, and worry far more than
we create visions framed within optimism.
Especially in today's fast paced arena of email,
instant messaging, and texting -so many have become
 spoiled by the luxury of modern technology that
keeps them "in touch". Yet with these tools has
come the expectation of a more rapid response
time and a higher demand for frequent contact.

57

Do you want to drive someone crazy?
Send them an email or text that just says;
"You know, I've been thinking..."
And leave it at that.
See what is said to fill the void of the unknown.
Nature SO does abhor a vacuum ;)~
And yes, I am one of those who believe that silences at times
says volumes more and speaks louder than any words.
AND at the same time I've been caught too many times
believing the silence meant something that it did not, and
it really was simply the amount of time it took between
the last words and the next. Darned assumptions.
Speaking of, don't ASSume for a moment that I'm going to
let you get away without including our Guest of Honor
where the issue of silence is concerned!
Yes, a refresher for some and fun for all -
the word is: ASSUME !!!!
And I'll skip the many definitions and just elaborate
on the one that I like & applies the most:
as·sume
"(1.) to take for granted or without proof; suppose;
postulate; posit: to assume that everyone wants peace. "

So let's flash back a bit at real Life scenario.
Some time ago a friend asked if I'd be interested in helping
work on a car, and I replied that I hated working on cars.
After several days, I asked them if they still needed help,
and they told me that they thought I didn't want to help!
I shared that simply because I didn't like to do something
didn't mean that I would not nor be unwilling to do it.
If I only did things I wanted to do,
I'd probably never get out of bed !

The ASSUMPTION that I did not want to nor was I willing to help cost them time, possibly money, and put a strain on the friendship. Another example. The other night another friend of mine was having a tough night and had shared a few things via text that were important to them.
Because I didn't reply immediately,
they assumed I "didn't want to talk about it".
Furthermore, because I "didn't want to talk about it" -
it was obvious that I didn't care about them or their feelings!
See? Isn't assuming fun ?!?!?
It's both fascinating and frightening
how often we fill in the blanks of Life.
One night someone I knew well told his wife "I don't care"
when she asked him if he wanted her to leave.
I think she assumed he was serious, and he assumed
she knew it was only said in a moment of frustration.
I'll bet you know what happened next. Yep.
Next day she was gone for good.
Ah yes, assumption comes at a price.
And I will never forget the lesson learned that night...

Let's look at a few more -
I don't want to assume you got the picture yet ;)
"My child is doing well in school."
Really? How do you know that?
Wait - Do you mean they're getting good grades?
Does it mean they are getting along with the other students?
Or is "doing well in school" mean functioning
in an acceptable manner in class?

"My spouse loves me"
How do you know that? Did they tell you that today??

"Well, no - I just know" OK... When did they last tell you?
"Oh, I don't know - it's been a while. But really,
  I don't need to hear it all the time."
But... How can someone in love with you NOT
want to share that with you and tell you often?
But if you were to ask him, he'd say that he washes her car
on Sundays, takes out the trash every Wednesday,
and leaves the fan on at night so she can sleep.
And in his world, that means "I love you."
Surely, she must know that... right ? Right ??!??

I've got to sidetrack a little, because
this is a subject near & dear to me.
WHEN IT COMES TO LOVE
(and you better believe this is all kinds of relevant)
Do you know what love is ? Do you know how to show it?
Do you know What makes you feel loved ?
I'll be honest, this has been a subject that has plagued me,
and unfortunately eluded me at times for years.
Because MY way of showing I love someone
may not convey nor be received as that -
just as THEIR way of "saying" they love me
may roll completely over my head;
lost, unappreciated, and unfelt.

I'm going to ruin your day here and tell you
that it's NOT the thought that counts.
I hope you chuckle over that statement,
and then I hope it sinks in.
A couple can continue thinking it's the thought that counts -
yet when they continually do not receive
that which says "I love you, I appreciate you"

THE WAY THEY NEED IT "SAID" TO "HEAR" IT

the happiness in that relationship is doomed.

Guys - have you ever had your girl say something crazy like

"You don't love me anymore!" ? And the best part is,

you could've just washed her car & waxed it -

even vacuumed the thing ! (I hate vacuuming, FYI)

Because, duh - you think she's the greatest and

you wanted to show her how much you care!!

But little did you know she had just got off the phone

with her friend Vivian, whose boyfriend had

just given her a bouquet of flowers. Translation:

Vivian's boyfriend cares about her and loves her.

You (boyfriend) are just lame and can only

think about cleaning the stupid dirty car.

You never give her flowers - you don't care.

(Note to self: in HER WORLD, flowers = love)

Good job, Casanova.

GUYS. (aka gentlemen) and GIRLS. (aka ladies)

Showing your love & appreciation

in a way that makes YOU feel good

DOES NOT guarantee that it will

make your partner feel good.

And when they don't get that what you are saying and doing

is your way of communicating your love & appreciation,

they will not react or respond accordingly.

Which usually sucks the winds out of the sails because

you were expecting the other to gush over how much

you must really care about them for you

to have said & done such a thing...

And... so you think twice next time you decide
to express how you feel toward the other.
After all - if they don't appreciate it, Why bother?
Guess how well this goes over with the truly beloved?
Do I need to go further,
or do you see where this train is headed?!?
Having been on both sides of this scenario, and
witnessing it among both friends and strangers alike -
there are no winners. And the talk around town is:
Guys are jerks, and girls are crazy.
Heard that one before ?
Now I know it must be some special kind of entertaining to
spend one's time trying to guess what their significant other
wants and needs to feel loved & appreciated.
Why else would people keep doing it ?
But let's imagine that we would rather spend our time
enjoying one another in happiness, and
travel that narrow path for a change.
Here's an experiment.
Name a few things that IN YOUR WORLD
make you feel loved & appreciated.
It doesn't matter what they are;
nor how personal and intimate.
Just take a deep breath, and write them down.
And at the end, write the following:
"What do I do and what can I do so that you
know beyond a shadow of a doubt how much
I love you, cherish you, and appreciate you ?"
I'm asking you to write it down because I think
 that this could be a very uncomfortable task
for some to try and discuss one on one.
Also - writing it down will help you to remember it :)

Heck - once you have "the list" carry it with you because
it may be the most important "to do list" you have!
Now, remember those 3 questions from early on?
Do you know what love is ?
Do you know how to show it ?
Do you know What makes you feel loved ?
It is important that you know the answers;
about yourself AND your partner - and make sure
both of you know one another's answers.
STOP ASSUMING that you know,
stop thinking you think you know.
Get the answers. KNOW !!!
I happen to think that Assumption kills more relationships,
sinks more businesses and creates more havoc and drama
than empty Silence. Silence rarely remains just that: Silent.
It gets filled with interpretation, assumption, and meaning.
A lot of frustration caused & missed opportunities
simply because no one bothered to get clarification
as to what was meant by the words that were spoken.
So, quick reminder back to the beginning:
(1) What you heard | (2) What you think it meant
Rinse. Repeat as needed until the words run clear.
Here are a handful of other questions that
can greatly chop through miscommunication:
~ "What did you mean by that?"
~ "Why do you say that?"
~ "Is there anything you'd like me to do about that?"
~ "How did you take that?"
~ "What can we do together to make this better ?"

Stop guessing and believing you're right.
There is great wisdom in the saying;
"The more I learn, the less I know.."

Don't allow pride to get in the way; don't get worked up
because it may seem like asking questions means you
don't have all the answers. A good indicator that this
may be a challenge area for you is if you just scoffed
at the notion of asking questions like the ones above.
So here's the deal.
This is a topic that cannot be talked about enough.
C O M M U N I C A T I O N :
It is the lifeline that connects us,
in virtually every aspect of our lives.
In my Life and in the lives of countless others I have
known and observed over the past decade, it has been
the number one source of the biggest breakthroughs -
and a lack of it the cause of the worst breakdowns.
Making it a priority to become clear in the communication
you share, with both others AND yourself, will change
your Life and will make a positive impact in the lives of many.
This isn't an opinion. I'm not sharing some theory.
My goal is not to inspire you tonight,
but to give you some tools and truth forged from
facts & findings collected from a 20 year journey.

So at the end of this, I now have a question for you.
How can making your level of communication more clear,
concise, and understood affect your Life and those around you ?

Be understanding and understood in your World...

DISTRACTIONS:
What Are You Looking Away From?

What if you woke up one morning and realized
that everything around you - everything that you and
everyone else thought was important, was there only as
a distraction to take your eyes off of something far bigger
and far more important to your Life and the lives of others
for generations to come. How would your Life change ?

Now, let's think for a moment about... just stuff.
Clothes, for example. Do you buy clothes because you've
worn them out, or more because you see some new fashion
or fad that tells you that you just HAVE to have them?
Is it more the looks, or the function??   Let's talk cars.
Do you drive a car because it is the most sensible choice for
your needs? Or... because it's fast or flashy? Perhaps the
grille or hood ornament makes you feel more... successful.
Maybe it more closely blends in with your neighbors...
Speaking of neighbors, why do you live where you do?
Because it makes sense, or because it shows "status"?
Does the interior of your house boast the necessities
or do you collect the latest gadgets, gizmos & "niceties" ?
How is that big screen TV, by the way?
Are you making sure you've subscribed to
every available channel, signed up for every available
download, and set your DVR to record any and all
shows that might've slipped through the cracks?
Step back from your "normal" life and consider that the
majority of your time & attention is devoted to distractions.

Take heed that the mainstream world is smiling at you,
nodding their head, and telling you that you are doing
the right thing - that you are being responsible,
successful, and living life as you should.

And not only are you working your lives away for it,
but so much of the time you end up spending the
rest your life trying to keep it or hold it together!

Ah, the glamour & the glitz; the shiny things that
turn our heads toward the sparkle of the moment.
How are these things building our future?
What are they doing for our children?
Who are you allowing to control this country by letting others
dictate your rights away - convincing you it's what is best for you??
Not sure? It's because you're not paying attention.
No... Hold it. That's not true.
Most of the time you are paying attention to those things
that are made to seem important. I'm guilty, too!
Crazy, though, what happens when you really dissect
the majority of the so called "important" events.
Most of the time they're merely minor things made urgent.
Entertained, content, and distracted.
Sort of like a mouse in a cage having a grand ole time
running nowhere on its little wheel. He's got food,
water, shelter; entertainment & amusement.
I'll bet he doesn't even know he's in a cage!
To the dimwitted rodent, it's Home sweet Home.
I've often remarked how the best trap is one
where you don't realize you're in a trap at all -
one that is created to look and feel
like some place safe, normal...

Home.

Now, my goal isn't to ruin your reality here.
What I would really like to do, though,
is shake the sands of your hourglass a bit.

Take a look at how much time you devote to
those things that entertain and amuse you but
add no real value to you or your family's future.
Now take a look at those things in your Life that
you are not pleased with, that frustrate you;
things that you wish were better.

Now, go back to your "amusement".
Aside from temporarily making you feel better,
is it really bringing you closer to a solution ?
Distractions: What are you looking away from?
My guess is that it lets you bury your head in the sand for a bit...
Sometimes more than a bit.

But that's normal.
Let me stress that: THAT IS NORMAL.
It's what we know, it's what's been handed down to us
and fed to us for more years than I've been around
by those we know and strangers alike.
And many would argue that "to each their own"
and that we ought to do and experience
those things that make us feel happy.
Sign me up - I do, too !

But not at the expense and sacrifice of my long term
well being, or upon the backs of those I love and
care about; or even those I have never met.
And that's the part that isn't "advertised".
The largest industries in our nation are geared
toward our gluttony for glitz & glamour and our
addiction to the quick & convenient.
We flock to the fun & festivities -
even at the cost of putting food on the table.
I've seen it time and time again - it is no exaggeration.
Speaking of food on the table, that is
also a part of the "quick & convenient".
And Convenience has trumped Common Sense.

Many years ago a document was written that, among
other things lost sight of and/or pulled out of context,
read; "Life, liberty, and the pursuit of happiness"

All 3 are important to keep in place, yet it would seem
our "pursuit of happiness" has become such a priority
that we have allowed both Liberty and Life to slip away.
What is not so clear to see is that
while we lose touch of Life and Liberty -
we will eventually find happiness wither away.

I'm not one to have a strong faith that politics are the answer
to what challenges we face. I believe the political world
AS WE KNOW IT is a distraction from factions and
influence who play both politicians and the people
they are supposed to represent as manipulative
pawns in a much bigger game.

Which is why I place such emphasis on YOU
being in control of your Life and
creating it the way You want it.

If we can help others see that YOU
call the shots and lay claim to your Life -
then more of You would rely less on Them !

I hope you'll take some time this week to take inventory
of your time and see if where you're spending it is in align
with the hopes and dreams you had and have for your Life.
Take note of what you allow to distract you and pull you
from those things that should be priorities in Life.

And remember -
being in control of your Life is rarely a casual affair.
If it feels like your life is on cruise control,
chances are you may not like where you end up!
Take the wheel and take control back;
be intent with the time and attentions in your Life...

Doing What You Like

My hat is off to the person who wrote this:
" You will enjoy true in whatever you do. "
Now, I'm not 100% sure what they intended,
so I'm going to go with the first thought I had:

The secret to success lies not
in doing what one likes,
but in liking what one does.

I heard a self made millionaire in his 20s say that
when I was in my early 20s. Now, if you can hold this
to be true – and practice it, then wouldn't it make sense
to pick an occupation that would better prepare you
to achieve goals and dreams you have as opposed to
merely settling for an occupation that you "liked" ?
I say this because of the countless people I have known
and meet who, instead of learning to enjoy a field or
endeavor that can bring them the wants and dreams of
their Life, they settle for receiving the bits & pieces
of it based on some career, job, or occupation
they have chosen because they "like it".

The vision I've often had is trying to explain to my son
who wanted desperately to have that new bicycle
that he couldn't have it because "Daddy likes his job".
And how my son could have gone to college
if only his Dad had only picked an occupation
that made sense instead of because he "liked it".

Remember that old song from the 70?s that went:
" And if you can't be with the one you love -
Love the one you're with, Love the one you're with "
(thank you Stephen Stills)
Yeah, it's like that…

So I would invite those of you who still believe that
it's never too late to change, to do just that.
Embrace something new, something different;
and learn what you can appreciate and enjoy about it.
(This could be said of people, too – FYI)

You will be met with an uncommon success
- by doing the uncommon…

Do you have $3 to spare?

A priceless lesson…

When I heard the tapping on the window, I froze.
It's dark out, and I had pulled off the road into an
empty parking lot of a closed service station to find
out what had fallen off of the seat next to me.
Now there's a guy from out of nowhere at my door.
I opened the door, and as I did he said;
"Do you have 3 dollars you could spare?"

I figured he was in his late 50s or so, and he looked…
well like someone who would be asking a stranger
for spare change in the middle of the night.
He also spoke in a manner that suggested that he may
have been born with challenges that most of us have
never had to deal with. For a brief second, I thought
about how much cash I had on me, and came up with:
$5 bill, $10 and a $20. So I said "Not tonight".

He thanked me and hoped God would bless me.
Door closed, he walked off into the darkness.
And… I began to wonder; $3. What an odd amount.
I was pretty sure I didn't have any $1 bills, but
(and this might sound strange) I wanted to keep
my integrity in check about it. So, I opened my wallet.
$10 bill. $20 bill. And (you guessed it) 3 x $1 bills.
I smiled. I asked my son if he saw where the man went.
He told me which direction, and we drove. Asking me why, and
I replied that I had found three one dollar bills in my wallet that I
did not know were there, so I was going to give them to the guy.

72

Now, normally – I don't have "spare money".
Tonight was no exception. Far from it!
However, I believe in a good cause.
And with it being so close to the Holidays -
I know every bit helps. So, back to tracking down our
stranger in the night. My eagle eyed son spotted him first,
so we pulled off the next road in front of him and waited.
I put one of my cards inside the folded over dollar bills
and walked over to him. I told him that I had checked
my wallet and had found the 3 dollar bills he'd asked for.
He seemed a bit surprised, yet undaunted - telling
me again that he hoped God would bless me.
And once again into the night he disappeared.

I really don't have a deep, meaningful message
to finish this with… yet. I'm not done !
But you know… It feels good to do the right thing.
It feels good to be your word – WITH YOURSELF,
let alone with those in your World.
That man never needed to know I had the $3.
As far as he was concerned, I was probably
like everyone else who lied to him and said "No…" .
But… I guess it's like that old saying:
"Character is what we do when no one is watching."
It's one thing to be true to others – and we should; yet it is
far more empowering to be true FIRST and foremost to YOU.

Little did he know that his words
would come true in such short time.
I was blessed, and am once again
by a man asking for a mere $3.

He should have asked for more…

Do You Know How To Fly ?

This is going to be short because
some things just don't take much to mean a lot.
We're riding in the Jeep (My 5yr son & I)
and all of a sudden he asks me if I've seen
the movie with Peter Pan but it's not really
Peter Pan because he's all grown up.
"Hook !" I shouted quite proud of myself :P

He then asked me what I needed to fly.
"...Uhhh... I don't really know - Do you ?" I responded.

Then he exclaimed (there really is a connection here)
"Pixie dust "
" and a Happy thought !!!"

and without skipping a beat he said:
"Mine is my Dad"

Son...
you are
and ever will be mine

~Dad

Do you want to be Friends?

We're sitting... let me correct that.
I am sitting watching my now 6 year old son
running and climbing on the play structure.
As I'm listening to the voices of the other children,
on two occasions I hear the words
"Do you want to be friends?"
asked by some small voice somewhere
amidst the frolicking kiddos.

And I got to thinking...
Is it really that easy?

What's the first thing that came to
your mind when I asked that?

When I asked that of myself, my thought was
"If only it were that easy".

Which led to the next one;
"Why isn't it?"
and
"Maybe it is... and we're just too scared to ask."

Many more questions, more analyzing, and more thinking.
Now I'm sitting here with you wondering what happened
between the time the child's voice asked
"Do you want to be friends?"
and now, where society seems to believe that it's just
not an acceptable question for mature adults to ask.

When was the last time you went to a social gathering
walked up to a complete stranger and asked
"Do you want to be friends?"

(...and I'm not going to wait for you to respond,
because I'm guessing it's never happened
since you were like... 4.)

So why is it we don't ask other people
"Do you want to be friends ?" ??

Is it because you have all the friends you need
and don't need to make any more?

Is it because you're too busy to make new friends?

If you're like me, the very notion of doing such a thing
brings to mind a vision of looking like a fool,
being laughed at, ridiculed, mocked, teased, belittled...
(it's a longer list I won't bore you with)
But here is the 2nd thing I realized as I watched
my son play with all of these kids who were
mere strangers just minutes before.

He expects the other kids to like him,
and he acts as if they will;
there's not even a doubt !

AND THEY DO.

The kid is my idol when it comes to social skills :P

So I'm going to repeat that,
because I think it says volumes.

He expects the other kids to like him,
and he acts as if they will.

He knows other kids want to play with him
He knows other kids will like him
He knows they will accept him

AND THEY DO.

I always believed the opposite when I was a child.
I didn't expect others to like me or want me around.
And I acted accordingly.
I was aloof, distant, anti-social, and avoided people.
It worked like a charm :P

So how is your Life working for you?
How are you approaching others?

Maybe you aren't exactly asking people
"Do you want to be friends?"
- but are you interacting with them
knowing that they want to be around you?
Are you believing that they like you?

My theory is that if we truly believed that other people
want to know us, want to be around us, and
would love to be our friend - without a doubt;
we would not be afraid to ask, nor hesitate.
AND our actions and attitude would do
the asking - even if we never did.

I have discovered the greatest secret
over the past few years;
it is a priceless realization the depths of which
I have not yet even begun to tap.

There are two amazing people here right now.
You
        and
            I.

And who wouldn't want to be
friends with someone amazing ?!??

So...
Do you want to be Friends?

There are some amazing people around you who do.

Feeding the Mind -
Food for Thought...

I'm looking at my bottle of green juice that I've been told
smells like grass and looks like grassy mud water.

And I got to thinking how much I've been spending
for the benefit of my health & physical well being.
Which then immediately turned to my mental health.

Guess what ?
I've spent more on education than I have on cars !
While this may not seem like a big deal to most, those who
have known me since I was a kid may raise an eyebrow.
After all, in high school - I lived and breathed cars !!

Still, I have spent more on the feeding of my mind.
That, and my brain has been on a stricter diet than most,
hence the selling of my TV in 1989 and only the rare and
sporadic viewing of it since. But don't worry - I'm not too
brain damaged; I still enjoy the occasional movie :)

Of course, what we should be clear on very early here
is that our minds are not malnourished in any way.
Oh no. Trust me - our minds are being fed well.
And in better stereo, definition and clarity than ever!

The bombardment of media from every angle fills our minds
at every opportunity with various "comfort food" to
entertain us, distract us, and keep us in line.

It's a topic far too vast for me to even touch on here.

So for now just keep this in mind:
whether aware or not - our minds
are being fed junk food for free.
So, I suggest you become more proactive about
the things you allow into your body and mind.

Now, let me ask you this.
What do you spend on the feeding of your mind ?
Wait. Wrong question. "Junk food" doesn't count.
Garbage in, garbage out.

Rephrase.
What do you spend on the positive, healthy feeding of your mind ?

I've driven & flown across both state lines and U.S. borders
because that's what I had to do to get the answers I sought.
I've spent thousands additionally attending lectures, courses,
training, seminars, and obtaining various educational materials.

I'm not saying it was an obsession,
but it was far more than a hobby. ;)P

The greatest gems of knowledge and pearls of wisdom
do not require being within the walls of a university or college.
I've found them from the experiences and sharing of
those who have gone where I've dreamed of going,
done what I've wished I could do, and
had what I felt was out of reach.

What would you be willing to pay for that ?

Just food for thought...

For Kids - *And Those Who Care About Them*

It was not quite 10 o'clock when I started out tonight.
I finally got the clutch fixed in the Roadster,
just in time for a few rain sprinkles :P
The top will have to go down another night...
So here's what I found next to the checkout stand at
the gas station tonight; "all natural Crayons sports drink".
In a nutshell, an energy drink geared toward kids.
Yes, the same kids whose raging sugar levels
cause them to misbehave in class,
exhibit the attention span of a 2 year old,
and set records for child obesity year after year.

I've been in schools and have been astounded
by what I've seen in the vending machines there.
Vending machines - that thought alone befuddles me.
Since when did kids become so lazy and spoiled ?
Oh wait - is it the kids or the parents ?
Let me get back to you on that...

From junk food, soda, candy and various "juices"
(ever thought about those 2 cups of sugar in Hi-C?)
the youth of today are the number one consumers
of what my parents used to call "junk food".
Just grab a bag of munchies - it's quicker.
Pop open another can of pop - it tastes so good!
How many aisles in your grocery store are now
devoted to snacks, candy and soft drinks?!?

There's BIG money selling us
what feels good in the moment.
And THAT is true across the consumer spectrum.
It's frustrating to know that the leading cause of
"supposed" A.D.D. can be traced to one's diet -
and in most cases can be drastically reduced if not
completely cured by a sensible food regiment.

Oh, it's easier to just put a label on behavior problems,
academic challenges, etc. That way all we have to do is
get a prescription, medicate America and call it good.
But since when has easier been better?
Of course, it's not just A.D.D. type symptoms that show up.
Do you have a child who has difficulty
getting around in the morning?
Behavior challenges?
Keep track of how late they're eating
and **what** they're eating.
Chances are if they are eating past 8pm,
especially junk food - they're not
getting a deep enough sleep.

Of course, you don't know what you don't know,
and if you didn't know this, well - you didn't know.
Heck - I know this, and I still eat way more junk food
and drink more pop than I know I should !
Hopefully having shared this will keep me
more accountable to my own health.

So, there you go.

My test drive turned into a tangent !

Nice....

Well, I'm going to toss this can of
bad tasting children's sports drink into
the trash and hope it's launch is a failure.
We don't need any more junk being piped
into the bloodstreams of our kids.
Have another glass of water kids -
you'll be thankful for it when you've
lived a longer, healthier life because of it

And for the rest of us,
only do it if you want a
longer healthier life.

Your call,
            your choice...

For Our Soldiers

A few times I've heard a commercial on the radio
about a program that sends letters to our soldiers abroad.
From what I gather it stemmed from the idea of a 15 year old.
Now I know there is a LOT of controversy about why our
soldiers are deployed, and it is a very charged subject across
all political lines. What I'm hoping for is that you can strip
away your current views & emotions on the subject.

I have a twin brother, and years ago he served in the military.
I'm trying to envision him in a far off country where many
of his fellow soldiers have lost their lives. I'm imagining
being in his shoes; feeling what he felt; the fear of
knowing I may be the next victim of war.
But I am a soldier, loyal to my country,
my family and to those I love.
I am here to obey and follow orders
because that is what is required to keep
my country free and my family safe.
It doesn't matter that I like it or not;
I've had many jobs I haven't liked !
But here I can't just quit - lives are at stake.
The future of freedom is what I risk by quitting;
and in the end the very lives of my family and all I love.
My life is worth that...

I wrote my brother occasionally, and I didn't find out
how much he appreciated my letters until
years after he was out of the military.
Had I known, I would have written more.

84

Looking back, I wonder if my brother eagerly looked
forward to the mail call of the day. (Do they have that ?)
I can just see him smiling as he was handed my letter.
I just know he'd be so proud - showing it off to his
Navy buds. More than likely he'd read it to a few;
out there even other people's letters were a
connection to home for everyone.
Of course, I'm a goofball - so they all probably
just shook their heads and felt really really
grateful that I wasn't their brother!
heh heh heh...
He'd fold the letter back up, put it somewhere safe -
knowing that he was loved and cared for,
and that would be enough.

So I'm thinking, what if there are those serving
this great country who go to sleep every night
never knowing that they are appreciated and cared for?
I think that is truly sad - after all they sacrifice for US...
The least we could say is thank you.
And we should.
Why not take a few minutes to write a letter to someone
who is putting their life on the line for you and I.

I'm sure there are websites you can find easily
that tell you where you can send it.
That's what I intend to do after I post this.
Sometimes I do actually listen to what I write ;p

So I'll leave you with this,
and it's something I heard nearly 15 years ago.

**"All it takes for the forces of evil to rule this land
is for enough good people to do nothing."**

It's going to be easier to do nothing.
Though I want to believe every one of you
would want to make a difference to someone
who has pledged their lives to protect our country,
I know it's so much easier to just let it slip away.
Just understand that our country became a country
- AND remains a free country today
because of people who did the right thing
instead of taking the easy way out.

Now if you'll excuse me,
I have a letter to write...

Giving Me My Dream

Some time ago I was at a friend's house
and a show called "Heroes" was on.
There was a point at which someone was asked;

"Do you want a life of happiness, or a life of meaning ?"

The question moved me to my core.
You see, I have known that answer for many years;
I just haven't embraced it and lived my Life accordingly.
Ever have that feeling there is something that you
should be doing in your life - With your Life?
And no matter what endeavors you undertake,
or ventures you pursue, at the end of the day
you find you've only managed to cover it up.

So here's the deal:
Have you ever experienced something that
you wanted to share, but didn't know how?
And what you really wanted to do is just tell the
other person to just do it and don't ask questions.
(ie: "shut up, listen, and do it !")
Yeah - that !!! OK - now it's my turn.
There is something that I'd seriously like you to do.
(Did I really say "shut up, listen, and do it !" earlier ?)
Go see the movie "Freedom Writers".
(Wow, I really did say "shut up, listen, and do it !" earlier !)

Out of the 168 hours you have this next week,
I'm only asking for 2 of them.
If it was important enough, you'd find them.

So let me do you a favor by saying it's important enough.
(Self test: - If your first reaction was an excuse
as to why you couldn't, take a look at
what other areas of your Life are affected
by excuses why you can't as opposed
to reasons why you should...)

I wish I could tell you why
it will be important to you, but I can't.
The best I can do is mention a few things that I went through,
which is just a tip of the iceberg that is my ever shifting Life.
Ironically enough, I was reminded of this just the other day
by a fellow co-worker who had said "I'm just a driver".
There was a kid who doubted his ability to win
an upcoming battle, and at the height of
his fear and doubt said to his 'trainer';
"I'm just a kid from a trailer park"
to which he replied
"If that's what you think, then that's all you'll ever be."
(from the movie "The Last Star Fighter")

Now here's where I'm torn,
because there are so many people and voices in our world
that are constantly telling us what we can or cannot do.
It drives me crazy and it makes me downright mad when
I hear anyone telling someone that they can't do something.
And I don't mean in an illegal sense, like a police officer
telling a 15 year old they can't buy cigarettes.
(by the way, if you smoke - stop.)
((No, really - stop.))
I'm talking about the people in our Life who,
in so many ways tell us we can't.

You know what I'm talking about.

Those who condemn our ideas or tell us it can't be done.

Usually it's the ones closest to us that have the most impact

- and so often it's subtle and delivered with love and care.

After all, they mean well !

But... I'm going to head another direction.

The truth of the matter is, has been, and will always be

that YOU are the stone wall in your way.

Let the others throw their rocks for now.

You are where you are right now because

you've grown content with the life you lead.

I didn't say comfortable

- I didn't even say you had to like your life.

What you have done is settle for it the way it is.

Like the old hound dog on the porch

who would howl every few minutes.

Come to find out, he was laying on a nail – but

it didn't hurt bad enough to make him get up and move.

From this day forth you can howl & whine to whoever

will listen - but until you get moving toward what you

want you'll never get away from where you are.

"If you keep doing what you've been doing,

you'll keep getting what you got"

(I heard that years ago from a well respected businessman.)

So - get off the nail !

Here is what I know and must come to grips with myself;

nothing is beyond my grasp or out of reach.

I've just simply given up too soon,

and accepted my own "I can't do it".

People... we are amazing.

Look around at all that we have accomplished in the world.

From skateboards to skyscrapers, the ingenuity of Man

continues to make new discoveries and reach new heights.

Yet individually, what can we do ?

We can move & touch, we can walk & talk.

None of us has been given a gift of magic;

to each we have been given every ability we need

to be able to accomplish whatever it is we set our heart to.

But you must set your heart to it.

You must pursue your desires with a passion

that only grows stronger with resistance.

That kind of passion is contagious, and you will find

that others will begin rallying to your cause.

You see, it wasn't until rather recently I came face to face

with the realization that one man can make a difference.

That is very different than saying one man can do it all.

I had the two thoughts meaning the same.

Bill Gates can do nothing more than you or I.

What he can do is direct others to utilize

their own thoughts, resources, and energies

into the fulfillment of his idea, goal, dream, etc.

People without obvious means or power have changed

the face of nation upon nation - people just like you.

I hadn't planned on this, but I am going to use myself as an example.

Currently I'm listening to "A Song of Simplicity" by Elijah Bossenbroek

- and it's repeating over and over. It's totally energizing and inspiring

me as I write. The day I meet this talented composer/pianist

I can tell him how his music kept me at the keyboard

where I was able to compose my own dreams.

That somewhere in my words there sparked
the desire in another to move beyond their walls -
to move in the world around them
so that their world would be moved.

Someone somewhere finally "got" that we are all equal
- that the only limits are the limits we place on ourselves.
Soon more and more people see the change in this person,
which inspires them to cast off their own self made chains.
Seeing this, my own dream unfolds as more and more people
lose the blindness of their abilities and discover their potential.
With confidence bolstered, I write and share even more
which results in my dream also becoming my occupation.
Passion feeds and grows passion, as more and more people
catch the dream and eagerly give what they have received;
from a neighborhood, across a city, spreading across a nation.
Would the world, too catch & embrace what we now know?
Could it be that an idea that I once scoffed at
and mocked would become a reality?
It can, and I believe it starts with you.

I know I started out wanting you to see a movie that holds
a valuable message, yet there is something else now.
Earlier I wanted to tell you that my answer to:
"Do you want a life of happiness, or a life of meaning ?"
was that I wanted my Life to have meaning
more than I wanted a life of happiness.
The reality is now that I know there is meaning,
there is a true happiness deep within that
nothing superficial could ever compare.

Thank you for giving me my Dream...

GO !

There are many people who will boast of the great things
they are going to do – who will share in earnest the mighty
deeds and glorious dreams they are setting out to accomplish.
I know – at times, I am one of them.
Tonight my observation is that inspiration
moves the heart and soul; yet it is
motivation that moves them to action.

There are a handful of people in my Life who I have
observed take their dreams and make them a reality.
People who have taken a leap of courage and acted
in spite of any walls and have created their own
windows of opportunity; Windows of opportunity
that so many of us simply wait and hope we will find.
I know – I am also one of them.
And rather than simply proclaiming their ambitions, dreams,
and goals, they plod forward with unglamorous action;
day after day – more often night after night.
For a while they may give up the fun, oftentimes
they will sacrifice wants - Understanding that immediate
demands are not necessarily important needs. And
what they are DOING will give them far more
reward than any such immediate gratification.
I know – I used to be one of them.
(insert awkward silence ;)P)

This past year I have shared with many that I am
my most avid reader. I typically say it jokingly and
yet it is true, no matter how odd it may seem.
There is a reason for everything I've ever written.
I don't always know what that reason is -
all I know is that it is there to be let out !
So I've spend many a sleepless night doing that.

Because what's been in the back of my mind for the
last 2 weeks is something I wrote in high school
that I've never really "heard" nor heeded;

"Go after what you want in Life
Don't let it pass you by
Never give up and be caught in strife
You can do anything if you try…"

The first word is the most important:
"GO" (meaning take action!)
followed by the first 3 words of the 3rd line:
"NEVER GIVE UP" (meaning keep taking action!!)
Now, if you'll excuse me - I have to GO… :)

What If You Gave Your All -

instead of just going through the motions?

There is a question that I must ask you...
And... I feel like it has to be just the right question
or else the answer - the real answer
will never be found.

So, I'm going to throw a few of the many not "right" ones
out there in an effort to find just the right one :)

What would you rather be doing?
Seriously - right now at this moment,
            what would you rather be doing?
                    Are you doing it?
                        Close??
I got to thinking about my own answer to that one,
and at this moment in time, I am thrilled to be doing
exactly what it is I want to do! Yes, at 2:36am in the
morning I am completely psyched to be writing to YOU !
The noise and distractions of Life are but a distant whisper
of the passing day; the chores and challenges past.
Now... I've got to tell you that, in a way it's a bit sad and
disappointing to say the least that the majority of our
lives are spent NOT doing exactly what we want to do.
The best hours of the best years of our lives
are rarely spent pursuing our true Passions.

Instead, we forfeit our freedoms and relinquish our rights
to the greater pursuit of Happiness in a desperate trade
for what we believe to be safety and security. Why?
And am I willing to be honest with the answer??

Well, to be brutally honest in my case;
it's just been easier to go through the motions.
Sure, I've tackled many challenges -
I've gone after numerous pursuits;
yet when the dust has settled and despite
knowing better - I've take the easier Path.
You... you really have to know how tough that is
for me to say to you. For years I've poured my heart
and mind into trying to convince YOU not to give up;
tried to tell You that the rewards in Life are worth the
struggle and pain to achieve. And for most years I've
been cheering you on from the sidelines; not the stage.

I'm reminded of part of a song I heard the other day by
Matthew West. Here is the part I heard that hit me hardest:

> " I don't wanna spend my whole life asking
> What if I had given everything?
> Instead of going through the motions "

This is very relevant to my thoughts,
so here are the lyrics in their entirety:

------- The Motions by Matthew West ---------
This might hurt, it's not safe
But I know that I've gotta make a change
I don't care if I break,
At least I'll be feeling something
'Cause just okay is not enough
Help me fight through the nothingness of life

I don't wanna go through the motions
I don't wanna go one more day
without Your all consuming passion inside of me
I don't wanna spend my whole life asking,
"What if I had given everything,
instead of going through the motions?"

No regrets, not this time
I'm gonna let my heart defeat my mind
Let Your love make me whole
I think I'm finally feeling something
'Cause just okay is not enough
Help me fight through the nothingness of this life

'Cause I don't wanna go through the motions
I don't wanna go one more day
without Your all consuming passion inside of me
I don't wanna spend my whole life asking,
"What if I had given everything,
instead of going through the motions?"
take me all the way (take me all the way)
take me all the way
('cause I don't wanna go through the motions)
take me all the way
(I know I'm finally feeling something real)
take me all the way

I don't wanna go through the motions
I don't wanna go one more day
without Your all consuming passion inside of me
I don't wanna spend my whole life asking,

"What if I had given everything,
instead of going through the motions?"
I don't wanna go through the motions
I don't wanna go one more day
without Your all consuming passion inside of me
I don't wanna spend my whole life asking,
"What if I had given everything,
instead of going through the motions?"
take me all the way (take me all the way)
take me all the way (I don't wanna go, I don't wanna go)
take me all the way (through the motions)
take me all the way
... I don't wanna go through the motions "

So... back to my first question.
What would you rather be doing?
What would you rather do on a daily basis that
you aren't doing now because, like me
you've settled for some easier path?
Another question:
What if you gave your everything - even if only for a while,
if it meant being able to finally pursue and obtain
the Happiness you truly desire?

Most people in this country (I'll say the average) have
chosen to settle for taking sips of what they want out
of life instead of going for the gusto & drinking deeply.
They live within a certain comfort zone, work about 40
hours a week, take a 2 week vacation sleep 8 hours a night.

They live for the brief freedom of their weekend,
doing those things that relieve the stress and
strains that they've spent the week creating.

Years ago I believed that the reason this
was the path of the "common" man must be
simply because they didn't know any better.

What I've come to realize is that most people,
even if given a choice and the opportunity
to change their situation will STILL
do the familiar and comfortable.
They go through the motions of Life;
they settle for what is given them
and rarely stretch themselves beyond
what they know and believe is achievable.

Like I've said before, it's always
easier to NOT do
something
than it is to DO.
With that I should add that it's far easier
to tell stories and create justifications as to
WHY we live our lives the way we do -
and how we're right to do so.
Now, I didn't say out loud - though I've heard
every excuse in the book from people as to why
they don't do the things in Life that would allow them
to achieve those things that they've shared they really want.

Typically the excuses & justifications are kept in the mind -
that way they aren't open for any debate that might require
contemplation, change, and possibly confrontation
with the man (or woman) in the mirror.

So... what I'm wondering now that we've made it this far
is that maybe we've lost sight of what we really do want.

This could be the greatest and most rewarding investment
of time you will ever make, and that is to take a few hours
And WRITE DOWN what it is that you want.

If you're really serious about it -
eliminate any and all limitations.
What I mean is,
don't base what you want on exterior circumstances.
It doesn't matter your current income, profession, career,
job, education, ethnicity, ability, history, background, beliefs;
nothing matters - you have a clean slate.

And on that note - I'm going to end this,
because I don't want to distract you from
taking the time to write down what you want.
Goals, dreams, ambitions, achievements;
            no boundaries and no limits...

Gone in 30 seconds...

30 years...

OK, I have a test - a very very simple test.

I'd like you to sit there for 30 seconds.

1 one thousand

2 one thousand

3 one thousand

4 one thousand

5 one thousand

6 one thousand

7 one thousand

8 one thousand

9 one thousand

10 one thousand

1 one thousand

2 one thousand

3 one thousand

4 one thousand

5 one thousand

6 one thousand

7 one thousand

8 one thousand

9 one thousand

10 one thousand

1 one thousand

2 one thousand

3 one thousand

4 one thousand

5 one thousand

6 one thousand

7 one thousand

8 one thousand

9 one thousand

10 one thousand

Do you know what I did in that 30 seconds?
I poured myself a glass of eggnog. (half milk & half
eggnog to be exact - because that's the way I like it)

Now I could have sat here with you and counted, but since
I knew the 30 seconds was going to be there I figured I'd
do something useful instead of just letting the time slip by.

You have no idea how long I've wanted to share that with you.
(No, not the eggnog part - FOCUS !)

You see, 30 seconds was going to come and go
regardless of what I did - or did not do.
So will 30 minutes, 30 hours, 30 days,
30 weeks, 30 months, and 30 years.

Now, you don't have to tell me this -
but what things have you always wanted to do
and just didn't have the time, money, know-how, etc.?
And - will you still be saying this in 3 years... and 30 years ??
That's like me wanting to play the piano.
I've wanted to play the piano since I was in
elementary school. 30 years have come and gone,
and my love for the piano remains; yet my skill and
ability to play are the same as when I was 8.

Really, people - the time it takes to learn, experience
and do ANYTHING is going to pass whether you
do something or nothing at all toward it's achievement.

Don't just let it slip by...

Push aside your excuses and actually DO something
that will get you just that much closer to achievement.

I did. You're reading it now. 30 minutes.

Feels good :)

Goodbye

Well, here I sit.
It's 3:12am and by the time I got home
I was almost ready to put off writing this.
Then again, there are many things
that are easier to put off than to do...

Tonight I played XBox with my brother & his neighbor John.
John moved to Washington from Florida several
months ago with his wife and 2 daughters.
Tomorrow he flies back to Florida to meet up
with the rest of the family, who went back
down to Florida before Christmas.

So let's make this story short.
John is one those people who
makes you feel welcome.
When he sees you & says "hi" - there is
no doubt the is genuinely glad to see you,
and makes you feel glad you were there.

Anyway, lest I ramble here - as we we're all leaving
my brother's, what I said to him was something like;
"Well, good luck with everything..."
and shook his hand.
It felt awkward.
I felt like there was so much more to say
- and I couldn't believe I was saying goodbye
as though it were any other casual "see ya later".

I watched him walk down the sidewalk, letting
the last opportunity to say how much I had
appreciated him fade away with the shadows.

Sometimes I wonder if "goodbye"s
are the reason I have so few "hello"s...

So John, what I never said was
thank you for always including me,
making me feel welcome,
and making me feel like
someone worth knowing

...and I'm sorry you never knew.

Don't let the "Johns" of your Life
walk away without knowing you care.
You may never know how much they need to hear it...

Boy meets Girl
They fall in love
Live happily ever after.
~~~ The End ~~~

So, this whole boy / girl / love thing -
let's skip past the first part (meeting).
Let's talk about the fall...

What I've observed is that the first months
of any relationship both parties are really
pouring on the charm & pulling out the stops
while at the same time throwing out little "tests"
for the other person to see how they'll react.
Over time, more testing, a little bit less of the
"pouring it on" taking place and a little more
catching up in the areas of life being neglected.

As a certain comfort level with one another grows,
it becomes important to gain a sense of balance.
Typically each person has been giving so much in
the beginning that they've lost a bit of themselves.
So, as comfort - even security- in the other grows,
so does the need to gain back the independence.
Part of the time and attention lavished on the
other may be redirected toward friends, work, hobbies;
things that were important before the new found love.
Things that more than likely were cause in creating
the person with whom we've become affectionate with.
To eliminate them would be to dismiss a part of
someone's life - a life we now care deeply for.

It doesn't have to mean that they care any less for us.
Now, as we move a bit more into our familiar environment
we can also begin to see a bit more objectively those
things about a person that might not be... desirable.
We can weigh these things more logically only when our
hearts and emotions are not as completely wrapped up
in the other person, as in the beginning stages.

Men will usually do this sooner than women.
And most women will react when this happens with
"What's wrong?" as if there is something wrong
and that this isn't simply a progression of most
any and every relationship throughout time.
The severity of the reaction is often a reflection
of how the woman perceives herself as a whole,
and the more fragile the self esteem is
the quicker "what's wrong" becomes
"What's wrong with me?".

Interestingly enough, when the woman is the first
to enter the more logical stages, she is typically
far more forgiving and tolerating than the man.
She far more likely to turn a blind eye to
many things that others would warn her about.
BY NO MEANS am I saying this applies only to women,
because I'll bet you could tell me stories of both
men and women you know who you just shake your
head and wonder "Why are they together?!?!?".
And if you're brave enough to ask them, you'll
get answers like "They're not that bad" or
they'll throw out some redeeming feature meant
to make the "red flags" not so red...

More like, let's say rose colored glasses...
Still, the fall slows.
Forces such as doubt, fear, uncertainty -
all pushing against the falling in love;
keeping the heart from committing itself fully.

And...
the question that keeps begging to be asked
Do we push forward, OR Do we push away ?

We all have our own scales that we weigh the
pros & positives against the cons & negatives.
If we accept a person for who they are,
Will these red flags and "flaws" plant
themselves and eventually take root -
causing a deeper resentment over time ?

Do we take the risk of pursuing the passion
with the hope that a love will grow that
might transcend & overcome any challenge ?
Do we look at the long term,
or do we live in the moment ?
Do we settle for someone we can live with,
or hold out for someone we can't live without ?
And how long do we search
before we decide to settle down... or settle for ?

Such a quandary...

So let me skip to the "Happily ever after" part.
Because I think the order is all wrong.

Let this soak in, because I think it will help.
The "chances" of being in and falling in Love
will increase a thousand-fold if you can let go
of believing that your happiness is and will be
determined by you being in love...

Happily ever after
boy meets girl
fall in love.

The End.

I'm sorry you had to wait so long to get to this part,
but the real gem in all of this is that if you are
looking for love and if you are expecting, hoping,
wanting love from another to make you happy -
that is putting a LOT of pressure on them !
And when people are under pressure,
they typically pull away.
And what will you do ?
You'll pursue !

STOP IT !!!

Stop letting your happiness
be determined by another.

Just
         stop.

Did you stop ?

OK, good.
Now that you have -
here is what you'll find.

The quality and caliber of people
who will be attracted to someone who
walks this Life creating and holding
Happiness within REGARDLESS of
where they walk or with whom;

THOSE are the kind of people
who would kindle and create
"and they lived happily ever after"

In addition, you'll meet some amazing people
and make a few friends along the way...

I should mention starting in the mirror :)

Happy New Year !
Resolve To Have One :)

So here we are: A New Year.

Now I know a lot of people around the new year have
spent time making resolutions to finding solutions
to things that weren't quite so right last year.
A new year - what better time for a fresh start, right?
Well, my optimistic friend - let's ignore the statistics that
show how many people do NOT keep their resolutions,
and never mind those nasty numbers that show a third
have given up before January has flipped its final page.
You and I will keep our blinders on as half of those
"other guys" fall out of the Resolution race!
But, before you dig in those new cleats -
I've got to ask you this question: What's different?

OK, I lied. There are several questions.
Yet they're all going after the same answer:
What's new about this year?
What's changed from last year?
What will happen this year that didn't happen last year?
Why will this year be so different than last year,
and did you say the same thing LAST year
about the year you just finished?

If you find your brain stuttering and stumbling for an answer,
you're not alone. I mean, let's face it - simply because we
turned a page on a calendar did not give us magic powers,
did not produce a winning lottery ticket, nor make us smarter,
better looking, stronger, wittier, luckier, funnier, or better.

Flipping the page from one calendar year to the next
gave us nothing that the day before didn't have or lack.
So now that I've completely let the wind out of your sails,
allow me to repeat the great news that
you just read and probably missed.

Flipping the page on a calendar gave us nothing
that the day before DIDN'T HAVE OR LACK.

I am happy - ecstatic really, that you honestly believe that
somehow this year will be THE year where things will be
different and that THIS is going to be YOUR year to shine.
Because that says you have hope that it can.
That's the spark. That's the first step!
Yet I want you to be crystal clear on this:
this new year ahead will not bring you
anything more than you bring to it.

The same brain and brawn that didn't see your resolutions
through last year are right here with you now.
Happy new year. Welcome back. Nice.

Again, the answers to those questions I asked earlier
are going to open up doors for you if you answer honestly.
Because if you do nothing differently, you will join
those 50% who have failed and/or given up on their
New Year's resolutions before July comes calling.

If you do the same things you did before
and follow the familiar patterns you know so well,
Why expect this year to bring you anything extraordinary?
YOU need to be extra UN ordinary
to make the extraordinary happen.

**Because if you keep doing what you've always done,
you'll keep getting what you've always got.**

Something to keep with you, and then I'll let you
get back to keeping your New Year's resolutions:

**The best things this year will be created by You,
a result of both what you do and how you are being.**

The numbers on a calendar do not make a year,
and moments in our lives are not marked.
Each come to us as the other -
to see what we make of them,
and what we are made of.

I wish you a very Happy New year,
and hope you don't stop at wishes -
but stretch yourselves to create
not only a great year,
but a great Life...

Healthcare "Crisis" Is Due
To Our Own Health Care

You know what's an interesting thought,
is that across the board the US can chalk up
the majority of its health concerns on a terrible diet.

I'm painting with pretty broad strokes here, and
it's not political (sorry) - but ignorance is not bliss
when it comes to preventative health.
It should be our first concern
and it IS our first line of attack
against the majority of what
ails the people of this country.

Of course, it's easier to pop a pill, get a shot,
have a surgery once our bodies have begun breaking
down from the fats, chemicals and otherwise pure trash
we've been pouring down our necks for years.
It's especially easier not to worry about when there is
health insurance to cover our every ache and pain -
and with a deep pocketed government guaranteeing
healthcare for everyone, why not sit around all day
and eat potato chips & drink pop?

Just like modern medicine -
we're always looking to "fix" the symptom after the fact.
We're not addressing the real cause, much like government
(you know I've got to throw that in there :)P)
and we keep mopping up the messes without
rolling up our sleeves and fixing the real "leak".

Want to have enough funds for healthcare?
Do you want to do your part to allow people
who NEED medical attention to get it??

Look in the mirror, look at what you are & are not eating.
Look at your weight (I know, SO not P.C.)
and look at your exercise, or lack thereof.
Oh, and this may be the most valuable piece,
and hardest because it requires effort.
READ.

I'm sure the whole 4 major food groups thing was considered
a big breakthrough in helping Americans eat healthier -
but in my mind it did more harm than good.
I see people reading ingredients and finding something
in those major food groups as part of the ingredients
in order to justify the purchase of it.
And they KNOW the item as a whole
is totally NOT good for them.
But it did list this so called "healthy" ingredient...
Brilliant.
When I say READ -
read up on what science, medicine,
and nutritionists have discovered about
food AND how it is processed by the body.

YOU
HAVE
O N E
B O D Y
TREAT IT LIKE THAT !!!

Did you know you shouldn't eat meats and potatoes together?
Yet what is almost a staple of the American "diet"?
Yes, meat and potatoes. It's a basic part of what we've
been told is a "well rounded" part of our dinner.
Did you know cooking, boiling & steaming foods
destroys most of their nutritional value?
Fruits should be eaten at least a half hour
BEFORE a meal; NOT for dessert.
AND did you know that even CHOCOLATE was actually
used for its healing and medicinal purposes long before
"we" Europeans got to it, destroyed it's nutritional value
and turned it into candy? Yep. But get the facts;
MOST chocolate isn't good for you. Find out what IS.

READ READ READ !

You'll probably have to go off of the "mainstream" media
to get the real facts that aren't biased by big bucks.
And when you're reading the ingredients label
at the grocery store, don't skim over the contents
& chemicals looking for the "acceptable" ingredients.
ie: Maraschino CHERRIES are not good for you.
BANANA cream pie - not good for you.
Finding "SPINACH" as a 5th ingredient after words
like "hydrogenated oil", "high fructose corn syrup"
(has the word CORN - must be good, right?),
"sodium nitrite" and monosodium glutamate"
is NOT a good indicator that what you are
about to eat might be good for you.

I'd say use common sense - but really,
you don't know what you don't know,
and we grab a box or can at the grocery store
because that's what our parents did when they shopped.

Commercials tell us that it's good for us,
and we should believe T.V., right?

I could go on and on here. No really, I could !!!
We haven't even touched the protective layering,
let alone the surface. Not to beat a dead horse
(every pun intended) but most people I see
put more attention, research and priority into their
home entertainment system, cable T.V. and cell phone
plans than they do into their own day to day Life.

The hospitals are full because we have for years
filled ourselves with junk, and the vast population
only seeks to gratify our pallet & gullet with things
that taste good instead of what IS good for us.

And, as most things I will ever talk about,
the solution rests IN OUR HANDS.
Not any government.

And it is OUR responsibility.

Leave the "problem" for others to "fix"
and you may not like the answers...

Hitting The Wall...

Do you sometimes find yourself
beating your head against a wall wondering
what you're doing wrong and why you can't get it right?
Let's take a break from head banging for a minute
and consider & contemplate this:

**"The same brain that
  got you into this mess
  isn't going to get you out."**

I heard that a few weeks ago, and it speaks such a clear truth.
How often do we try to figure out why things are the way they are?
How often do we speculate, investigate, and otherwise invigorate
our brain cells to come up with THE answer - THE solution
that will make our Life the better that we hope for?
(clue: MOST OF THE TIME !)
How is that working for you?
Maybe good, maybe not so good. So so. NOT.

You view your Life with the eyes of what you know.
You see what you are looking for instead of what IS.
You do not know what you do not know
because you do not know you do not know it!

When you think you know it all, you have set the walls
within which the answers can be found, and the potential
that once existed in this vast Universe has been shrunk
down to the 3lbs of grey matter between your ears.

There is a reason the greatest sages throughout time
have shared in so many ways that the key to knowing
is at first admitting that you know nothing...

Humbling, isn't it?
Almost as terrifying as it is enlightening.

Aside from this piece of good news,
even though you may not know the answers;
the answers may very well be within you to find.
Remember that vast Universe I mentioned that
held the answers and solutions you seek?
Guess what? You're a part of it !!!

One way to look at it is this.
Ever tried putting together a puzzle from one box
while looking at the box lid to another puzzle?
I'd ask you to try it some time, but I think
you know how it would turn out!
You'd end up beating your head against a wall!

And that's what you're doing when you think
you have the solution or know the answers.
You're looking for pieces of the puzzle
that look like the picture on the box.

So always keep an open mind
and be open to finding solutions
that may not look like the answer you had in mind.
You will find you have far more options than you thought...

How Do You Want To Feel?

Several weeks ago I had fallen quite hard
while running on snow covered concrete.
Not a brilliant thing to do.
Since then both my elbow and shoulders have been a
constant reminder of what happens when moving
body parts meet an immoveable object at high speed.
Like most people will, I've been taking it easy,
and lately it has occurred to me that I am acting
like someone who is injured. I'm moving slower,
noticing every pain from those areas and reducing
those movements that cause discomfort.
You know how it goes...

Now, In my early twenties I had the great fortune
of being introduced to the minds and thoughts
of some very extraordinary people.

And like it was yesterday, I heard these words today;

"If you want to FEEL enthusiastic, ACT enthusiastic!"
(Thanks Zig :))

I heard this while I was walking across the room.
And almost instantaneously, my own words echoed;

"If you want to FEEL healthy, ACT healthy !"
In that instant, I took charge of my health.
I straightened my back and walked taller,
and I no longer felt the pain I've had.

I moved my arms and at most experienced the ache
that comes with not using them on a regular basis
- not the deep sharp excruciating pain that I've been feeling.
For the rest of the day I felt fantastic!

Now, those of you who know me know that I like to whistle.
I feel happier when I whistle !
For many many years when I've wanted to feel better,
I would start whistling - and I do that to this day.
Same thing.

> "I do not sing because I am happy,
>
> I am happy because I sing"
>
> (- William James)

Now, I have a recipe for you and I.
But first, 2 questions :)

How are you feeling?
How are you acting?

If you're like most people,
you probably react to how you're feeling.
You receive news that makes you mad, and
chances are you'll be/act mad to varying degrees.
AND... the longer you do that,
the more that feeling will persist.
Something happens to make you feel sad,
and you begin to do things that sad people do.
Guilt... Anger... Grief... Helplessness...
These and many many more are emotions that
typically carry with them a set of behaviors
that we tend to carry out as if programmed.

What I have noticed in most people is that
these feelings, though normal reactions & emotions
- are kept in play far longer than need be.
And yes, oftentimes it is because of
the attention received from others
- but that will be a topic for another day.
Just keep in mind it takes a certain kind of
brutal honesty with one's self to discover that little fact...

All right, to those who are still reading
you remember that old phrase
"You don't know what you don't know" ???

If we don't know how to break out of the
downward spiral of emotions that cause our reactions
which further feed our emotions; then we just don't know,
and we simply let what happens happen.

Eventually time will pass,
(does it heal all wounds, really?)
and emotions will fade until eventually
we come back to some form of "normalcy".
BUT IF we know that action affects emotion,
then that puts the control in our hands.

Now, I am not saying that you should
put aside your emotions and pretend
that you aren't feeling what you're feeling.
I am not telling you to "Fake it til you make it".
Our emotions serve us and are there for our health.
To deny and stuff them over time leads to worse problems.
You know this to be true.

What I am saying is that if you want to stop
being overcome and controlled by these emotions
- then start taking steps to slow the fall.
Here's a good start that ALL of you know:
"Laughter is the best medicine".
Science has known this for years.
Put it to use !!!

Now, I know it's hard to find something funny
when you can't see through the tears,
and it's tough to smile through
the gritted teeth of anger.
Still, if you truly wish to overcome
being overcome by your emotions;
you can and will once you are ready.

Let the healing and strengthening attributes of
your emotions run; just don't let them overrun you.
You will continue to feel how you act.
If you want to be happy, act happy.
If you want to feel sad, act sad.
If you want to feel productive, do something useful.
If you want to feel joy, do something for someone else.
If you want to feel compassion, comfort someone in need.

There are countless things you can do
to put yourself on the road to feeling
how it is you WANT to feel.

...and now you know :)

How much do you want ?
and...
How much do you settle for ?

So I'm in the shower, and it occurs to me
that in the past week I have been approached
3 different times by people who were in need.
(of course these thoughts happen in the shower!)

One person at the gas station needed to get
up to Seattle and needed money for bus fare.
Another kid needed a taxi ride up to Woodland, and
the last person simply asked if I had any spare change.
"Spare change?" I replied to him.
I told him that none of my change was really "spare" -
because I typically trade it in for cash when it accumulates.
So I took the change from my pocket -
there was almost $3 jingling around in there.
While he watched, I counted out 75 cents - because
that's how much those air / water machines cost,
and I figured if I needed them I'd have them.
Those were not "spare".
I let him have the rest.
And...
I walked away thinking how much
he had short changed himself.

You see, the other people had asked for money to
fulfill a certain need. To each of the others I had asked
"How much do you think that would be?"

123

To the one who needed a taxi cab, he wasn't sure,
so I gave him all I had in my wallet minus $2.
The $2 was not "spare" - I figured it was enough to
buy me a bite to eat later. It wasn't much - maybe $7.
The other kid said he just needed a couple of bucks,
so that's what he got.

What I've found fascinating about all of this,
is that each of them got what they asked for.
Yet I don't think any of them got what they needed.
In every case, they began asking for a minimum amount,
and expected to receive even less.
And what I've discovered in Life is that
we typically receive that which we really expect.

I give all of them kudos for taking the initiative to approach
a stranger and ask them for anything, let alone money.
Whether they be in need or just greed -
that's a "skill" that many people don't have.
Still... they really short changed themselves.
Just like I do.
Just like...
you do.

My 5th grade teacher was Mrs. Wilson.
She told my brother one time "Never sell yourself short".
I'm pretty sure he had shared this with me back then,
or at least I heard about it later.
What I can tell you is that in my case,
it was rarely heeded or applied.
And from what I've seen from those around me,
they've either never heard it or ignored it !

Yet, more than that, I can't help but wonder if
it isn't simply that we don't realize that we are
selling ourselves short... short changing ourselves.

Now, just so you know - I can tell that
I'm not going to like a lot of what I say here.
And... I'm going to say you / me / us a lot.
Don't take any of it personally -
but do take everything to heart :)

How many of us sell ourselves short in what we do ?
How many of us short change ourselves
in what we earn in our occupation ?
How many of us settle for less in our relationships ?
How many of us take what happens to come our way
instead of going after what it is we truly want ?
How many of us accept that today will resemble yesterday
and tomorrow will probably be a repeat of today ?
Same ole, same ole...
Another day, another dollar...
Same $hlt, different day...

Do you know why ?

Because you're asking Life for spare change,
and you're expecting & accepting pennies on the dollar.
You are NOT asking of Life what you are worth,
and you are asking far less from yourself.

So here's the scoop –

we're going to talk about you from here

on forward because I already know I do this.

Heck, I've got it down to an art form - if not a lifestyle.

SO I KNOW IT WHEN I SEE IT !

And I see it in you.

You are asking so much less

than what you have to give;

You expect so little of yourself

from that which you have to offer.

Mrs. Wilson would be disappointed...

Because what I'm sure she saw those many years ago

was the unlimited potential and untapped abilities

of that young pupil before her.

It's a lot like the miracle

      I see before me

           when I look

                at you.

How To Save A Life

How would you feel if you saved someone's life ?
No, really. Quit "multi-tasking"
and give this some serious thought.

Picture whatever scenario you want to:
Pull a person from a burning building
just before the roof caves in.
Perform the Heimlich maneuver
on a child who was choking.
Push someone out of the way of a speeding car.
Pull a drowning person from the water
and revive them with CPR.

There are so many ways to save a life –
but I want you to choose one that's real to you;
a situation that you can actually imagine yourself being in.

The feelings you have seeing that their life is in danger.

What you feel when you realize
you might be able to help them.

When you make the decision to act.

While you're rescuing them.
How you feel when they're finally safe from harm.

When their eyes meet yours –
and you both know that they
are alive because of you.

What if you were invited to the hospital where
they were recovering. You see their family and
friends – their hearts overflowing with gratitude.
I mean seriously – you're getting handshakes and hugs
from strangers - many with tears in their eyes,
thanking you as much as words can say.

Now what if…
What if saving someone's Life wasn't as spectacular
as pulling them from a burning building, giving CPR,
or stepping between them and harm's way ?
What if it looked more like a sincere word of encouragement
to someone who was down on their luck & out of hope?
Maybe it came from a teacher who tells a student
that she sees amazing potential within them.
And it could be as simple as saying
 "It's really good to see you".

When people of any age lose faith, give up hope, or
lose the desire and passion that gives them purpose;
Life becomes more of a daily drudgery than a precious gift to savor.
And when one's life is deemed cheap, decisions are often made
to dull the pain and find quick & easy pleasures, which all too
often lead them into a lifestyle that results in an early grave.

Let's face it – we live in a world that practically screams:
"You're not good enough !".
And with this thought ever beneath the surface,
many people's lives are cut short either by their
own hand or circumstances created by poor choices.

Remember Newton's Law:

"An object in motion will stay in motion and an object at rest
will stay at rest unless acted upon by an external force".

BE the external force
in someone's Life that causes them
to veer from their course of destruction.

DO what you can,
no matter how small or seemingly insignificant,
that might uplift or lighten the burden of another.

SEE outside of your self
and look around at the opportunities that surround
us daily to make a powerful and positive change.

Kindness and encouragement are a key ingredient in keeping
many people on a path of longevity and a healthy lifestyle.
Now, the part that might be standing just around the corner
is this: The Life you save may one day be your own.
You may have to take my word for this one, as
I'm sure most of you do not feel as if your life
is in any danger nor are you in need of help.

And for the handful that "get" this –
thank you for being among those hands
that have kept me from falling along the way,
and for listening to that still small voice inside that says:
"Do it now"
        when you see the chance and hear the call…

How To Solve Your Problems

Many years ago I heard someone say
something that I'll never forgot.
(slightly paraphrased after 18 years)

> "If you want to solve your own problems,
> find someone else with a bigger problem,
> help them get over theirs, and all of a sudden
> your problems won't seem like such a big deal !"

And you know what ?
It didn't happen overnight –
but tonight it dawned on me that
nowadays I don't get so hung up on all
of my faults, shortcomings, failures, inadequacies...
(There's a longer list - but I didn't want to bore you)

For much of my life these things have ruled me
and dominated so many of the decisions and
directions I've made since I can remember.

As I've devoted more energy and time toward others,
the majority of junk & garbage that for so long seemed
to capture much of my time and attention is now finally
on the back burner - instead of the other way around.

Now THAT... is cool.

No, that is beyond cool.

Because I always thought I needed to
get my own life all squared away and
perfect before I could start trying
to help others in a meaningful way.
Turns out I've had it backwards all this time.

                              pleH

                       srehto

               evlos

        s'rieht

...tsrif

If Only Life
Were a Rehearsal

It's funny the things I find when I'm looking for other things.
Like this that I jotted down back on June 25, 2009.

Ever seen the movie "Click" ? I watched a bit of it tonight
until I got to a certain part, and then I had to leave.
I made the excuse that I had to go to the store.
The part I'm referring to is where Adam Sandler is in
his office, and his son, following in his father's footsteps,
is trying to go over a few of his ideas with him.
But Adam is too busy checking his email to pay attention.
Next, in walks his dad, who tries to invite him on
over that night to have a sort of boys night out.
Not only does Adam ignore his dad, but he then
lashes out at him for interrupting his work.
The dad, deeply hurt, says:
"I'm so sorry I barged in; I love you son..."
as he reaches out and touches him on the head.
This scene is from the past, and it is a piece of
the past revisited by the son - because it is the
last time he ever sees his father alive.
Adam rewinds this scene of his life again and again.
And at the final replay, freezes the moment in time
and is tells his father in a voice quivering with emotion;
 "I love you too, dad..." and he kisses him on the cheek,
and then says; "I'll miss you... ...you know that. Goodbye..."
Of course, I had to leave at the "I love you too, dad".
There are some things that just cut me too deeply to the core.

Wouldn't it be great to be able to go back in time and
fix the wrongs - to make things right where we blew it;
Or fast forward the parts we didn't like ?
Wouldn't it be great if this Life were just
a big rehearsal of some screenplay ?
We could edit the parts we didn't like,
go back, re-shoot until it was just right.

I often think that's the way many of us live our lives.
Like... this isn't "it"; we've got time to get it right.
Up til now it's just been... "practice".

Dare I say even that today doesn't really matter -
there's always a tomorrow; we'll deal with things then?

sigh...
What you can't see is
that I've been sitting here
trying to write this for nearly 3 hours.
Sure, there are distractions around me -
throwing me off track, losing my thoughts...

But then I keep seeing that scene where
the last words to a father were:
"Can you let me do my work?!?".
And in watching it again, I see that his
grandfather's face as he's walking out
the door is wrapped in anguish and pain.
And the next scene a graveyard... a tombstone...

You know... I've often shared how important
it is to tell those we care about how much
they mean to us; how special they are.

I guess as I'm sitting here I realize that
although these words are written to you,
in my heart they needed to be heard by me.
Sometimes....
there is just so much I miss
that is right before my eyes.

After all, this Life of ours is both
the opening curtain and the final act;
and every line a moment
  we can never take back
      nor will we ever get back.

If People Were More Like Dogs

Just as I opened the door to the machine shop, the sounds -
very LOUD sounds – of barking dogs meet my ears, and for
a moment I wonder: Will I be a customer today… or lunch ?!
The four legged carnivores met me, tripping over themselves
trying to see who was going to get the first bite or nibble in.
Oh, but I recognized these dogs - they might be over 3 feet
tall on all fours, but they're all puppy on the inside :)
I LOVE DOGS !!!
Of course I start petting on them & patting them -
driving them further crazy. I think I was about to say
"There's a good girl" when the inevitable happened.
Yep. Uh huh. Excited puppy kisses met an open mouth.
It's all fun & games until someone gets a tongue in the mouth!
About that time another human finally enters the scene.
Buzz kill. We were having so much fun !!! Anyway.
He called the dogs off, I gave him the inlet from my
brother's paintball marker and we chatted about
how to remove the screw that had broken at least
one drill bit so far. You know – boring stuff.
SO NOT cute puppies !

After I left and got in the Jeep
(Lots of thinking happens in the Jeep, FYI)
I marveled at how I wished people were more like dogs.
Yeah yeah yeah – I'm sure there are bumper stickers
out there saying this very thing. But really; sometimes I do!
I mean come on – less than 2 minutes,
and a tongue in the mouth?!
There's something to be said about that ! ;)~

Now I don't know dog-speak,

but I figure as soon as those dogs

saw me I'm sure they thought:

"There has GOT to be something fun about this guy

and we are going to find out what it is !" followed by:

"And if there isn't, we're going to make it fun anyway !" -

all the while lot's of:"Look at me! Look at us! Stay there !!"

I know, probably not the best interpretation,

but again - I don't know dog-speak !

The experience made me think of the time I was at

an indoor play arena with my son and while he played

on the play structure I heard more than once;

"Do you want to be friends ?" uttered by some gleeful child.

Most of us (mature, grown up adults) are just so… stuffy.

At what point did we go from being accepting, loving and

open with others to just being sticks in the mud?

I think we need to hang out with puppies and kids

who aren't afraid to ask for friendship -

and try acting like we're genuinely happy to

be with the other people who share our World.

Who knows – it could be contagious,

and wouldn't that be an amazing way to live!

If Tomorrow Never Comes

It's 2:30 in the afternoon.

I'm at work, and my boss gets paged to the phone.

The sound of his wife's sobbing voice is at the

other end, telling him her father has just died.

Brain aneurism - no signs, no warnings;

breakfast in the morning as usual.

As usual.

Lately I've been playing a song that really moves me,

and it's meaning echoes louder today than ever.

"If Tomorrow Never Comes" by Garth Brooks.

Ironically enough, it was the song I chose the other night

when I went to a bar to sing karaoke (see previous blog).

The lyrics are as follows - please don't just browse over them.

" If Tomorrow Never Comes "

Sometimes late at night

I lie awake and watch her sleeping

She's lost in peaceful dreams

So I turn out the lights and lay there in the dark

And the thought crosses my mind

If I never wake up in the morning

Would she ever doubt

the way I feel about her in my heart

(chorus)

If tomorrow never comes

Will she know how much I loved her

Did I try in every way to show her every day

That she's my only one…

If my time on earth were through
She must face this world without me
Is the love I gave her in the past
Gonna be enough to last
If tomorrow never comes

'Cause I've lost loved ones in my life
Who never knew how much I loved them
Now I live with the regret
That my true feelings for them never were revealed
So I made a promise to myself
To say each day how much she means to me
And avoid that circumstance
Where there's no second chance to tell her how I feel

(chorus)
If tomorrow never comes
Will she know how much I loved her
Did I try in every way to show her every day
That she's my only one
If my time on earth were through
She must face this world without me
Is the love I gave her in the past
Gonna be enough to last
If tomorrow never comes

So tell that someone that you love
Just what you're thinking of
If tomorrow never comes "

The song tells of a man wanting to be sure
his woman knew how much he loved her.
Yet to me it speaks of anyone
and everyone I care for.

If tomorrow never comes,
does my Dad know how much I love him ?
Does he know how much I appreciate him ?
Does my Mom ?
Does my brother know that he's the knot
at the end of my rope when times are tough ?
Do they really know how I feel about them
- and have I told them and/or showed them lately ?

Now you're sitting here reading this.
Some of you I know.
Some of you have touched me in areas of my Life
that I have never experienced; never even dreamed of.
I hope... no, I pray you know how much you've meant to me.
To you I've never met; Life is too short to be a stranger.
We have something to offer one another,
and neither of us has to know what it is now.
Live as though there is no tomorrow.
Easy to say, makes sense; rarely followed through.
I'm not even going to suggest that you live your Life
as though there were no tomorrow because it is
an undertaking that for most would involve
uprooting their entire life !

I just want to tell the people I care about
(which includes YOU) how much they mean to me.
It sure would be great if you did the same
- and did it with the intention that
the people in your Life
know it without a doubt.
I'd say tomorrow would be a good day to start, but...
well, you know what I'm going to say about that.

~in loving memory of Eric Steffen,
Becky Howe & Terry Stutzman...
my brother... my Friends...

If you can't say something nice -
Don't say anything at all?

"If you can't say something nice,
don't say anything at all."
My Mom used to say this when I was a kid,
and I was again reminded of it the other day while on
the phone with someone who had very little nice to say.
So what's a kid to do when faced with this directive?
Better yet, as adults - How should we handle it??

Here's an idea:
Instead of biting our tongue
and muttering under our breath,
let's use our energy and time
toward a more productive result.
Let's find something nice to say something about.

Now, this is going to take effort, and
for some people who have a complaint
about everything and anything - this is
going to take some REAL work !
And... they're going to complain about it ;)P

But seriously - finding fault is easy,
and constantly finding fault and looking for
the negative in Life is a sure way to keep it coming.
Those who do it the most are typically
those who find fault within themselves first.

I would suggest to them that the first place they start
to look for something nice to say is in the mirror.
Once they begin to see the good within themselves,
it's going to be a whole lot easier to see it in others.
Also, if you can forgive a few of your own "faults" and
stop being so hard on yourself - you may find it easier
to relate to and see why others do the things they do.

So this thing my Mom used to say -
what a fantastic challenge to throw down !
I'm not so sure she meant it that way, but if you
really take a hold of it and make it your battle cry -
it's going to seriously change the way you live.
Why?
Because it forces you to go beyond seeing the
easier things to find and discover the hidden treasures
that you've been missing NOT because they weren't there
but that you're too busy looking at what's wrong - not right.

My challenge to you is instead of picking
the "don't say anything at all" part of this -
step up, dig deep, and speak up !

You will make a positive difference in all our lives...

If You Had One Shot

"Look, if you had one shot, or one opportunity
To seize everything you ever wanted; One moment -
Would you capture it, or just let it slip?"

It's been 6 years since this song hit the scene;
"Lose Yourself" by Eminem.
So let's get one thing straight -
this whole "If you had one shot";
I want to know how many of you believe this.
"Look, if you had one shot,
or one opportunity To seize everything
you ever wanted; One moment -
Would you capture it, or just let it slip?"

I'm thinking a LOT of people can look back and recall
where they had a chance, an opportunity that could have
changed their lives. And I also know that some people
will say they've never had an opportunity in their Life;
that they can never seem to get a "break".
Most, I think, are secretly hoping & waiting.
For those not completely cynical and bitter who have
not given up hope that your Life will turn around and
your ship will come in - I'd like to ask you why you're
still looking for that one shot, that one opportunity.

I appreciate your optimism, don't get me wrong. But…
if you're limiting yourself to this one magical moment
where all your dreams come true -
no wonder you haven't found it yet.

Opportunity rarely exists within the walls we build,

nor is it often cloaked in garments of familiarity.

Not to be dismissive nor cast down on anyone's intelligence,

but we all too often look for opportunity thinking & believing

we know what it looks like. So that's why 'm going to start

out being disagreeable to the lyrics I started with:

"If you had one shot"

If? IF ?!?!?

And only ONE shot?!???

Well, if you're only looking for one shot,

no wonder it's going to be hard to find.

My guess is you're passing by countless other

opportunities as you're looking for your "one shot".

(unless you're just hoping & waiting it will come to you)

" IF ..." Come on, really???

So let's run with this whole thought.

"Look, if you had one shot, or one opportunity

To seize everything you ever wanted; One moment -

Would you capture it, or just let it slip?"

The good news… Scratch that.

The GREAT news is that there ARE more opportunities

surrounding you than you even know what to do with.

> **That you do not recognize them**
> **does not mean they don't exist.**

Like so many things,

they are merely

out of YOUR sight –

out of your vision.

It's like you and I sitting at a coffee shop,
and you ask why I'm drinking out of a cup.
Because you're sitting across from me,
you do not see the handle.
So, in your world,
it is a cup – not a mug.

If you rely only on what YOU see
and what you perceive in Life,
your vision will always be lacking.

OK. Here is the bad news. (Back to the lyrics we go.)
This part here: "…Would you capture it, or just let it slip?"
Oh, I KNOW THIS ONE !!! PICK ME !!! PICK ME !!
 "Let it slip" is the correct answer. 99% of the time.
Because most of us try to "capture" opportunity with a
fishing pole, at best. Now, when I think of the word capture,
I think of a wild untamed beast that doesn't want to be caught.
Enter: fishing pole. What do most people do?
They just throw the line out there and
run like heck away from the beast !
And they sit in the corner, hoping & waiting.

Dictionary.com says:
"CAPTURE: "1. to take by force or stratagem;
take prisoner; seize: The police captured the burglar. "

145

So let me boil this down and save you some time.
I probably should have just started with this so you
could get back to whatever it was you were doing.
(Who knows, maybe fishing ;)P)

One shot or one thousand shots
they will ALL continue to slip by
until you hunt them down
and capture them.

And whatever thoughts
and voices might be in your head
right now that are convincing you
that this really doesn't apply in your case -
are the very things
that keep you blind...

I Like The Way It Hurts

A while ago now I caught the opening lines to a song:
"Just gonna stand there and watch me burn
that's alright because I like the way it hurts…"

For those of you who know the rest of the song,
or even know what the song is about -
you'll have to forgive me:
this is the only part I heard.
It's all I needed to hear.

"Because I like the way it hurts…"

I think that's why a great many people choose
to stay down and accept their "circumstances".
They have reached a point where pain and failure
have become comfortable & frequent friends, and draw
to themselves in word and deed those things that would
cause and create the supposed circumstances that hold them.

Probably not what you were expecting me
to say about this part of a song, huh?
I warned you - it's just a few words pulled out of context.

"Because I like the way it hurts…"

As strange as it sounds, it reminds me of a canker sore I had.
It stung & hurt whenever I ran my tongue over it – and yet at
the same time there was a sort of comfort in it after a while.
Sort of a pleasure in the pain, if you will.
(No, I am not a masochist)

I think you and I both know people who seem to bounce from one "drama" to the next – always in some kind of turmoil. Yet it doesn't look like they're trying to mess their life up on purpose really. But if you pay attention to their speech you'll find so many little things said that work to erode any sort of real happiness. And so many of their actions cause them to trip back 2 steps while trying to move forward. "Because I like the way it hurts…"

I saw a sign recently that said "Soar to New Heights".
(I think it was in front of a church)
Now, at first – I'd think that sounds great !
Heck yeah – soar to new heights, count me IN !
But you know, there are many who would,
on a deeper level, find that a scary proposition.

SOAR to new heights? I can barely crawl…

NEW heights? I can't even handle what I've got!

HEIGHTS ?!?!? I fall all the time now -
it's only going to hurt more from higher up !

Best just to stay put,
because really -
I like the way it hurts.

Besides -
It's comfortable
I know it well;
it's familiar.

Interestingly enough, tonight I can use myself as an example.
It's been several days now since I first heard those lyrics,
and do you know why you're only now reading it ?
Thanks to distractions & procrastination,
I've had plenty of good reasons and excuses
that have kept me from writing you – and kept me
from sharing so many things from you. And somehow
the frustration & guilt of not doing what I know I should
be has become a tolerable if not enjoyable pain.
Perhaps I am a sort of masochist after all.

"Just gonna stand there
and watch me burn
that's alright because
I like the way it hurts…"

So… This isn't something I really wanted
to face or confront at 2:30 in the morning.
It should be interesting to see where it goes.
You know, it's really too bad you couldn't weigh in and
share a bit with me right now. I mean, I see the evidence
of this in others A LOT, but I don't think they see it.
I often wonder if you do. It's… a tough thing to bring up.
I mean, how do you say:
"Hey, did you know that all this X and Y stuff   that keeps
"happening to you" is because YOU keep making it happen? "
(Because you like the way it hurts)

People tend to get all defensive when you break the news
to them that they are responsible for their lives. I know –
I'm a people, too ! Speaking of people, I didn't want to
bring this up - but it needs to be said, so I must.

I had a friend once who was what many would consider...
Well, let's just be honest & say it plain and straight; a whiner.
Now you that know me understand that I am a "fixer".
You tell me you have a problem, and my reaction
is to try and come up with solutions & answers.
Took me a long time to really "get" that sometimes
people just want to share & be listened to;
to know you care and will hear them out.
NOT TO BE THEIR SAVIOR & FIX IT ALL !

But let me digress.
My friend... Long story short, she always had complaints -
always whined and woe'd about them to people.
Silly me stepped in and started fixing them.
And... I created a new set of problems.
She was running out of things to whine about!
No longer could she receive the sympathy and the attention of friends,
family & others. The very means to which she gathered and gained her
sense of importance – even love - was being taken away from her.
Not long after she found reason to fade into the sunset.
I wish her well...

So, back to the burn.
I think we should find out what you like about the hurt.
What does it give you that makes it worth keeping in place?
And if you can be honest with those answers,
ask yourself is it really worth the cost??

Because I really don't want to stand idly by
as you burn yourself time and time again -
professing that you "like the way it hurts"
when it's coming at such a high price...

I Miss You

I keep thinking about her handwriting...

We would often write each other notes & letters
- the good old fashioned kind with real paper and ink.
I loved her handwriting.
Her office was next to where I worked,
which is how we met over 11 years ago.
I'd see her during the day when she'd walk by.
We'd smile, share a few words - and it was always
enough to make the day a little brighter for us both.
It's funny - but we talked about how we needed
that little "pick me up" to make it through the day.
I guess you could say we just sort of clicked as friends.
Never will I forget the first (my only) symphony we went to.
I, as debonair as can be in my best suit - with her in a most
stunning burgundy evening gown. I think we turned a few heads!
We shared fun and sad times; moments
that create friendships for a lifetime.

She left the company she worked for, and like so often
happens with people who we don't see as much;
out of sight, out of mind.

It's been a few years since I saw her last.
Not long ago - a few months at best I kept thinking
I should get a hold of her & catch up on old times.
While I was moving boxes out of storage a couple
weeks ago I came across a letter of hers, and in
another box a photo she had taken of me and
a coworker of hers at her wedding reception.

A few days ago Heather, a friend & fellow coworker
of Becky's found me online and wrote me because
she thought she recognized me from where I worked.
Small world !
It had been about 4 years since I had seen her last...
Anyway, among other things,
I mentioned that I'd sort of lost track of Becky.

So here's the tough part of this,
and if it takes me all night to write so be it.
It's just that it's tough to see the screen through tears.

Heather told me that Becky had passed away in July;
and I just can't stop thinking about her.

I hear her voice, and I keep seeing her name
signed at the bottom of a letter...

'Becky'

We hear every now and then
that we should live today
as if it were our last;
that we should tell those in our life
how much we care for them.

Take it to heart.

~ for Becky, taken from us by a drunk driver 07/16/2006...
        I miss you...

In Another's Shoes...

Many years ago I heard a story about a letter that
Abraham Lincoln had written to one of his generals
during the Civil War. From what I recall, the general
had been hesitant at a time when immediate decisive
action was needed to achieve a victory, and because
of his delays and decisions a defeat seemed eminent.
The letter from Lincoln was harsh, and I suspect that
had the general received it would have probably resigned.
But the general never received the letter. It was found
after Lincoln's death, locked away in a desk drawer.

We may never know the real reason it wasn't sent.
Those who understood Lincoln theoried that,
after writing the letter, he stepped back and
tried to put himself in the general's shoes.
There he imagined the heavy casualties of the battle,
and what it would mean to give the orders that may
only result in casualties and death without victory.
And in that frame of mind, and in those "shoes"
he folded up the letter and locked it away -
for he better understood better the general's actions.

I make decisions that are influenced by my knowledge,
which is a collection of my experiences as well as the
experiences of others along with the many ways I have
"educated" myself through the years.
Just like you do.

Along the way, one of my "saving grace's" in watching
other people making decisions that affect their lives
negatively has been this revelation:

I would have done the same
if I were in their shoes and
experienced their Life as they had.

We all see people do things that drive us crazy,
make us mad, sad, and leave us shaking our heads.

Guess what ?

We've done a few things that have made others
look at us and think we're crazy, dumb, mean, etc.
(Trust me - many more where these came from :P)

So next time you are about to cast judgment, or
form an opinion on any matter regarding another;
try this first.

Take a penny from your pocket and ask yourself
" What would Lincoln do ? "

Chances are, the same as you...

Independence Day

(aka the 4th of July)

Independence Day:
a Declaration of Independence is nothing unless
we continue to ACT independent of our government.
The same holds true today as it did 233 years ago.

If our forefathers could see what we have done
with the liberty their lives have paid for,
I wonder if those brave revolutionists would ever
have signed the Declaration of Independence -
knowing that it would be their death warrant.

With the rights we have been given,
comes the responsibility to keep them
and practice them for ourselves
as well as our fellow citizens.

When we become lazy and begin taking the attitude
"it's not my fault - not my problem" and expect a
government to fill the void where hard work,
helping hands, and compassion should be -
in time that same government will completely rule us.

Day by day, we are allowing one form of tyranny
to replace the one that we are this day celebrating
a Declaration of Independence FROM...

As I've said before,
and will continue to say now more than ever:
this country was made great by WE the People
of the United States of America -
not the government in rule.

So this Independence Day weekend
I hope that you will do more than
support foreign communist governments
with vast fireworks purchasing and take a
moment (better a lifetime) to remember
what it was that our forefathers died for
and what generations have continued
to bleed and perish to keep:
Our Freedom FROM a controlling government.

Interpretation

Interpretation.
It's automatic; it's what we do with what we see, hear and feel.
Someone sneezes; we interpret it "must not be feeling well".
A painful look away in the midst of conversation;
"why won't he look at me - what's wrong ?"
A clerk hastily rings us up and barely says thank you
"what a &#%!!!" we think to ourselves... ;)

I know I've been wrong about my interpretations enough
to suspect you've been and are still in the same boat.
The key is in realizing that everything IS interpreted - and
then taking the time to find out if how we're interpreting
something is how it was intended; the "reality".

Unfortunately, I think we're too smart for that.
It's quicker & easier to just "know" what something means.
And yet this "knowing" is based on *our* past experiences.
If you and I get the feeling we're not understood, or have difficulty
in relationships, be it friend or other - we may want to look at
how we interpret other people; their actions, what they say, etc.
Sure - we'll draw a conclusion about everything.
But take the time to find out from the other person
what THEY meant; why did they say what they said,
did what they did, and so on.

Care enough for yourself and the other person to clarify.
It will surely bring you a life of greater happiness AND
eliminate a great deal of pain, stress and anxiety !

...and I think I'll start listening to my own advice ;)

I See Great People -

only they don't know they're great...

Last week I'm at the store walking around an aisle
when all of a sudden, a line from the movie
"The Sixth Sense" pops in my head;

"I see dead people, only they don't know they're dead."
(paraphrased version - I haven't seen the movie in 7+ years)

To which my mind echoed back this,
and it's been haunting me ever since:

"I see great people, only they don't know they're great..."

Do you know why it has taken me all week to write this ?
Because I don't know how to convince
someone who doesn't already know it.

And... if you could see me right now, you'd know that
I've been sitting here for the last half hour staring at
this line and not knowing the right place to go with it.

"I see great people, only they don't know they're great..."

Do you know what people who
don't know they're great do ?
(Here's a short list of examples)

They major in the minors.

They "sweat the small stuff"

They turn mole hills into mountains

They blame others for their lot in Life

They often feel helpless and victimized

They allow circumstances to dictate their future

They prioritize entertainment before accomplishment

They repeat failures and consider successes "luck"

They don't think things will get better (for them)

They stumble, they fall, and they stay down

They follow failure rather than seek success

They live reactively instead of proactive

They watch the news rather than make it

They play small in the game of Life

They complain... a lot...

They give up easily

This is a very short list - trust me.

And believe me, I've tried all of these and more at least once !

I also suspect a few of you could raise your hands if I

asked you how many of you have done any of these.

It's very frustrating to see people accept this way of Life as normal.

After all - you must know people who are just... well, great !

And yet they're living a miserable life day after day,

and at best, they settle for the table scraps of happiness.

At the top of my website you'll find this phrase:

"There is nothing of tangible significance

that separates the most successful

from the most desperate."

Nothing.

NOTHING.

N O T H I N G .

And though you and I are different and unique from one another;

we are capable of doing and achieving what any other has done.

Now, when you read that -

I want you to pay attention to the words

and thoughts that are running through your mind.

If they begin with anything resembling "Yeah, but" -

or any other kind of excuse or reason;

THAT is what holds you back, my friend.

You.

Not your capabilities or abilities.

Not your luck, or lack of it.

Not your upbringing.

Not your any thing.

Y O U

Now there is an uncomfortable place to be.

Because there has always been a reason to be where you are.

Sensible, logical, believable reasons why you are where you are.

So when anyone asks why your Life is the way it is,

you can hold up one of many "flash cards" and say

"This... is why"

And we can all nod in agreement and say
"Ah, yes - that makes sense..."

But... take away the flash cards,
and it's kind of like standing naked in front of a crowd.

Without all of the reasons
& excuses to hide behind,
everyone can see
that it's just you,
and nothing else.

Step out from behind that which hides you;
the magnificent and amazing YOU !

Accept that you and you alone
are the cause and creator
of the Life that you lead,
and every step from here forward
you will one day look back on
with either pride or regret.

Learn to see great people,
and begin by looking in the mirror...

I Shall Pass This Way But Once

" I shall pass this way but once;
any good therefore that I can do,
or any kindness that I can show
- let me not defer nor neglect it,
for I shall not pass this way again. "

Where I originally found this quote I do not know,
but I do know it was nearly 20 years ago.
I wrote it out and made several copies.
One went on my desk, another inside my planner, one
in my wallet, and taped another to the dash of my car.
While going through some boxes after my last move,
I found the copy I had on my desk and I came
face to face with the realization that I was doing
very little in my Life that would indicate
that quote meant anything at all to me.

The 2 lines that grab me the most are the 1st and last.
To me it means I am here now -
right now, and this is it -
there is no 2nd chance.

The middle describes purpose - my purpose.
Over the years I have subscribed more and more
to the theory that we are here merely to live our
lives and do what makes us happy... US. Me. I.
It explains why I've felt so empty & unfulfilled.
For those who know me - really know me;
I am happiest when I am helping others.

When making a difference - causing a positive
impact in the life of another; I am alive.

So here I am, writing to you... and writing to me.
What can I do right now - what can I say now that
will leave us both glad we shared this moment ?
Oh, but if I could read your mind at this moment...
You know, I'm reminded of a piece of a poem I wrote:

"To risk, to dare - to take a leap
we struggle with trembling fear -
for those precious words still left unspoken
are the ones we long to hear."

The precious words I spoke of here were "I love you".

" I shall pass this way but once;
any good therefore that I can do,
or any kindness that I can show
- let me not defer nor neglect it,
for I shall not pass this way again. "

There are those things that we hide from even ourselves;
secrets so deep that we remain blind to them.
Could it be that the reason I refuse to stop writing this
is because I... love you ? Is this the force that has finally
pushed its way to the surface tonight - past the denial,
past the fear, past the rationale & logic...

163

" I shall pass this way but once; "
I will tell you this now no matter
how foolish it may seem -

" any good therefore that I can do,
or any kindness that I can show
- let me not defer nor neglect it, "
You are loved. By me, by those
you know do - and many more.

" for I shall not pass this way again. "

You and I will soon part ways.
What I will leave you with is my secret.
I am afraid that you will not return the love I have for you,
and therefore I hide it from you - and never tell you.
From time to time I let it out in little pieces;
a kind word, a good deed, a helping hand...

                                    Then I disappear.

          " I shall pass this way but once;
          any good therefore that I can do,
          or any kindness that I can show
          - let me not defer nor neglect it,
          for I shall not pass this way again. "

Is It really That Bad?

What is the one area of your Life
that seems to be causing you the most problem?
How big of a problem is it?

For many months I've wrestled with how to get some perspective
on a concept that that could alleviate so much frustration and
unhappiness for people, and at the very least help create a
better understanding and appreciation for how we value Life.
With that much pressure, it's no wonder it's taken me so long.
How ironic that what initially inspired it
was the taking of one's own Life.

I don't even know if you can put your mind in this place,
but can you imagine creating a plan that would ultimately
lead to your death? I'm talking about the end of everything
as you know it and will ever know it - by your hand.

Now I am not trying to paint a morbid picture here,
nor is my goal to depress you or upset you;
but I really need you to step onto this stage
and put yourself into this role of The End.

So I want to repeat these two questions, and
I'd like you to keep them in mind until we part ways.

What is the one area of your Life that seems
to be causing you the most problem?
How big of a problem is it?

I would wager that if you were to have asked most of
the nearly 40,000 people whose problems were so big
to them that they chose to end their lives last year,
they would tell you that what they faced was
so overwhelming that it overcame and
overpowered their very will to live.

And THESE TWO WORDS are the most important
to take away from possibly this entire page:
> **TO THEM.**

It's easy to overlook someone else's problem as no big deal.
It's fairly common to shrug off what we don't think is
anything to get upset with and worked up about.
Give them time - they'll get over it.
They will see how silly it really is.
Like a marble.

Hold a marble in your hand, and for the most part
it's a rather small and insignificant thing to see.
Yet bring that marble closer and closer to your eye,
and it appears bigger and bigger - eventually
becoming the only thing you can see;
completely overwhelming everything else.

And you wouldn't see the answer if it was only 2 steps away.

You and I see people who get stuck by things
that we simply shake our heads at and say "Why?".

What we so often fail to ask is WHY it is
such a big deal TO THEM, because
we're too busy discounting that it is.

And perhaps, we're just a bit too distracted by
our own seemingly insurmountable walls to see
that no matter what the "walls" are made of,
they still serve to contain and control us.

YOUR challenges, situations, and problems
may seem quite easily solved by some of
the very people you look at and wonder
"Why don't they just (insert solution here)?!?!?"

What I hope you see above anything else
is that other people's situations are
just as real as yours **- TO THEM.**
Just as yours are - **TO YOU.**

Wouldn't you like other people to listen to you
and try and understand what you're going through?
Wouldn't it be nice to know that someone else cared?
On top of that, how fantastic would it be if they actually
took the time to step out of their own "stuff" in order
that they could help you out with yours?

YOU KNOW THAT WOULD BE GREAT !!!

So, how about doing that for them first?
* Never underestimate the power of:
"Do unto others as you would them do unto you".

It will come back to you,
whether in the form of what you'd hoped,
or in a way that is completely unexpected...

Is THAT How You Took that?!??

Some of you... No, wait - ALL of you are going to laugh and or
groan when you find out what my fortune cookie said tonight.

" You should enhance your feminine side at this time. "
I know.
I KNOW !!!
It's 2am and I don't know whether to laugh or cry about this.
I should cry, because wouldn't that be a great way to get
in touch with and enhance my "feminine side"?!???
Really, who went on break at the factory that makes these cookies?!

OK. So, now that I've allowed myself to think enhancing
my "feminine side" is a bad thing; I wonder in what other
areas of my Life do I perceive things said as being negative.
For example, I see women as a far more social creature; talkative
and outgoing. I've wanted to be more of THAT my entire Life !
But instead, I had visions of needing to trim my nails, pay more
attention to my hair, wear sweeter cologne, and maybe even buy,
oh, a dozen pair of shoes ! You can imagine my relief; although
I may buy a pair of shoes in the next month. (No heels - I promise!)

But you know, really - how often when people say something
to us do we immediately focus on the "what's wrong" of it
rather than the "what's right" ? Instead of taking things
at face value and as an opportunity to have a positive
experience and outcome; all too often we go to the defensive,
get our blaming finger out and begin pointing fingers with one
hand and building walls around ourselves with the other.

One of my favorite things to say when I hear the negative
reaction of another at something that either myself or another
may have said is; " Is THAT how you took that ? "

Of course, it's far easier to do and say for others
because being on the outside looking in you can
more objectively see the "what was said" and
then see what the other person made it mean.

Very often there is a HUGE difference between
the intent of a message and the interpretation of it.
For example, you're going to go to dinner with your
significant other, and you see what they're wearing.
What you say is; "Are you going to wear THAT tonight?"
(prepare yourself for a myriad of responses like the following)
"What do you mean? Don't you like it?? What's wrong with it ?!??
Does it make me look fat!? Why don't you ever like the way I look??
I can never make you happy can I ??? You don't even want to be
seen with me, and you just don't love me anymore - admit it...
FINE! You go out - I don't want to go anymore.
Maybe you'll find someone cuter out there who DOES look good.
You're such a jerk. Don't even come back. I hate you... "

And the response to all of this is:
"It's supposed to really cool off tonight,
and I was worried you might get cold."

Interpretation. Intent.

So let's do this. I'm not going to paint my nails
any time soon, but I am going to be even more
aware, open, and receptive to what others say to me.
And instead of jumping to conclusions,
I think I may start asking a few questions.
I think the best one would be;
"How did you mean that"
and perhaps even
"Why do you ask ?"
Heck, maybe you should try that today, too - I think you may
be very very surprised at some of the responses you'll get.
And if you REALLY want to have fun with this –
pretend as if the person who said it to you
actually cared about you, liked you,
and wanted what's best for you.
And if some of you really really like challenges;
try "hearing" everything that is said to you
as something that could make your Life even
greater than it is now, and be grateful it was said.

Now if you'll excuse me,
I've got to do something manly,
like work on the car or drink some beer,
maybe watch a sporting event. (Fat chance)
Heck - maybe I'll drink beer AND work on the car.
Maybe try swearing.

Because after that,
I might just buy shoes...
:)P

It Feels Good To Give.

Are you ready to receive?

It feels good to give. Doesn't it ?
Oh sure, sometimes we give out of guilt or obligation;
heck, sometimes we even do it as a way to manipulate !
But few things make us feel as good as when we give
unconditionally from the heart. And especially warming
is when we are able to contribute to the life of one
who is often giving to others themselves.

Now, this is something I've touched on before.
I've spent my whole life always trying to be the one who is
helping others and never asking for help - never allowing others
the chance to help me; not giving them the pleasure and good
feelings that are associating with knowing you helped someone.
When people see you struggling - and they care about you,
it is a GREAT feeling to be able to give back to them and help them.
I've never given people the chance. Like many people, I've always
held onto the notion that it is a sign of weakness to ask for help.
I can take care of myself - and shouldn't rely on others.
The real truth of the matter is that the most successful people
you'll ever meet became that way not by doing everything
themselves and relying solely on their own abilities, talents,
etc; but by asking for and receiving help from others.

And I'll just say this once before I move on;

Pride will all too often imprison you and prevent you
from being all that you could become,
and doing all that you could do.

So under the guise of being strong and stoic, I've ripped others off from one of the greatest rewards they might ever receive from me. BUT I have a win / win solution. Ready ? Now, don't let its simplicity undermine its power. Let's agree to try this for 2 weeks: When you need help, Ask. Yep. That's it. BRILLIANT! Simple.

And don't toy with me on this - don't just ask one or two
people who you know would help you no matter what.
That's playing the same game you've been playing, and
You already know how that's been working for you.
Step out and ask for help **until you get it.**
It may help to know that each person you ask is a new opportunity
for a solution and one step closer to the answer - AND they don't
know if you've asked one other person or 200 other people.
All they know is YOU are asking THEM for help.
And guess what? There are billions of people on this planet !

OK, one last thing before I cut you loose -
because I know the thought has crossed your mind.
Yes, you are.
That's the answer to the unsaid thought that is;
'I'm not worth it -- nobody is going to help me...'
Again - let's try something different.
Pretend as if they will, and that they want to
AND have been waiting to. Consider also that 2 weeks
is going to come and go whether you do this or not.
You have nothing to lose and everything to gain !

And a word to the wise and wishing to be so:
Quitting IS an option, but you've done that before
and it hasn't got you anywhere... right?
Again, try something different.

It's not about the singing

I remember I had bought candy bars for the other kids in class
the day they had the school dance. (back in grade school :))
I left the candy bars on their desks, and tape recorded
the dance while I hid under a desk - afraid to go into
the gym where the dance was being held.

This might give you some clue to how
afraid of people I've been in my lifetime.
A few years ago my son's mother convinced me
to sing karaoke at the bar of a casino we were in.

" Attack that which you fear and the death of fear is certain"
I remember I had to sit on a chair because I was shaking so bad -
and I had to hold the microphone with both hands.
The song I chose was "Oh Donna" by Richie Valens :)P
Not sure why, other than it was the first song I both recognized
and liked on the list. Did I mention yet I had a few drinks?
Dare I mention that we'd been taking courses that dealt with
overcoming fears?? Yeah... that might help. So, I did it.
The most terrifying experience of my life.
The only thing that came as close
was the 2nd time - later that year.

Fast forward to present day.
The sinking feeling in my stomach as my name is called.
The sweat that begins to form on my upper lip as I stand.
I begin feeling numb as I walk in front of all the people.
It is still terrifying. I take deep breaths to calm down,
knowing that in a few moments I have to sing.
Too late to turn back.

I play the song in my head, read the words on the screen and
try to make what comes out of my mouth resemble what I know.
My eyes never leave the screen, as my voice quivers and shakes.
One hand holds the microphone, my fingers resting against my chin.
It's the only way I can keep it steady. My other hand is in my
pocket to give the illusion that I am not as terrified as I am.

" Attack that which you fear
and the death of fear is certain"

The song is over, followed by polite clapping.
I head straight for my seat - seeing no one.
My heart is racing a hundred miles an hour,
and it is all I can do to pretend like I did not
just escape from a life and death situation.

If you haven't tried this, you should.
And not just for the reasons I've given :)

You should do it because you're sick and tired
of letting fear dictate what you do and do not do.

You should do it because you've let too many opportunities
slip away that you'll never get back because you were afraid.

You should do it so you can stop wondering
what might have been had you only _____ ...
(you can fill in the blank)

You should do it so that your Life is filled with
fewer regrets and more joyful memories.

You should do it
so you'll just stop
being so stopped.

And this has nothing to do with karaoke.

I heard someone ask long ago:
"What would you do if you knew you could not fail?"

Whatever your answer is to this question, I suspect
that fear has and will keep you from achieving it.

So my challenge to you: Face the music;
find the "karaoke" in your Life.
Press forward in spite of the fears
that would convince you otherwise.
It will make a powerful and positive impact
in virtually every part of your Life.

Let me know how it goes :)

" Attack that which you fear
and the death of fear is certain"

Just When You Think

There's an old phrase that goes something like:
"Just when you think things couldn't get worse..."
Today's reminder of that happened when I went to the
Bank and found out that I had $396 in overdraft
charges on my now very below zero bank account.
TIP: don't trust a phone call to get your account balance,
FYI: gas purchases don't register until some crazy later time.

So, that might not seem like a lot of money to you,
but to me it represented the loss of a Christmas gift,
two client's worth of website work, and a car payoff.
Oh, and 15% of today's direct deposit of my paycheck.
What bothered & shook me the most was that to me,
the bank took away something that was given to me
by people who mean a lot to me as well as
something that I had worked hard for.
Now, if you've read my earlier writings, you've got to know
that there is no way that I am taking the time to gripe
& complain about how unfair and cruel this is.
Of course... I am still upset about it,
but that's way better than the very crushed
and devastated feelings I had earlier :)~

About 15 years ago I heard a very wealthy man
jokingly say something very wise.
"No matter how bad you think you've got it,
there's always somebody else who's got it worse."
(Thanks Bill !)
Not sure about you, but I've spent a lot of time and energy
lamenting about that which I do not have, have not done, etc.

"I cried because I had no shoes
Until I saw a man who had no feet."

So, tonight I spent a few minutes looking
for people who "had it worse" than I do.

Helen Keller - deaf blind mute
Franklin D. Roosevelt - polio
Ludwig van Beethoven - deaf & asthma
Michael Bolton - deaf in one ear
Stevie Wonder - blind
Ray Charles - blind
Andrea Bocelli - blind
Elizabeth Taylor - asthma
Bob Hope - asthma
Kenny G. - asthma
Billy Joel - asthma
Liza Minelli - asthma
Axl Rose - bipolar
Julius Caesar - epilepsy
Richard Burton - epilepsy
Isaac Newton - epilepsy, stutter
Tchaikovsky - epilepsy
Elton John - epilepsy
Neil Young - epilepsy
Robin Williams - ADHD
Stephen Hawking - Lou Gehrigs Disease, ALS, paralyzed
Thomas Edison - deafness, learning disability & diabetes
(I didn't list the long list of other famous people with diabetes.)

And here's a short list of people you may recognize that
didn't let their dyslexia dictate what they could or couldn't do:

Agatha Christie - English mystery writer

Albert Einstein - Scientist, philosopher

Alexander Graham - Bell Inventor

Bruce Jenner - U.S. Olympic Gold Medalist

Charles Schwab - Founder of investment brokerage

Cher - Entertainer, actress

Danny Glover - Actor

George Burns - Actor, comedian

Greg Louganis - U.S. Olympic Gold Medalist

Hans Christian Andersen - Author

Harry Belafonte - Singer, actor, entertainer

Henry Ford - Inventor, humanitarian,

Henry Winkler - Actor, director, humanitarian

Jackie Stewart - Race car driver

John Corcoran - Real estate millionaire

Leonardo Da Vinci - Renaissance artist, sculptor, painter

Lindsay Wagner - Actress, author, "The Bionic Woman"

Magic Johnson - Professional athlete

Nelson Rockefeller - Former governor of New York & vice president

Nolan Ryan - Professional athlete

Ozzy Osbourne - Rock music star

Quentin Tarantino - Film director, writer

Thomas Edison - Inventor, scientist

Thomas Kean - President of Drew University, former N.J. governor

Tom Cruise - Actor

Tom Smothers - Comedian (Smothers Brothers)

Walt Disney - Cartoonist, founder of Disneyland/Disneyworld

Whoopi Goldberg - Actress

William B. Yeats - Poet, dramatist, Nobel prize winner

William James - Psychologist, philosopher

Winston Churchill - Former Prime Minister of Britain

Woodrow Wilson - Former president of the United States

So, tonight I had dinner, and I didn't have to stand in
a food line to get it - or worse, not have any dinner at all.
I am sitting in a heated residence typing:
there is shelter, heat, electricity, phone, my son is with me,
AND he has HotWheels that he got for Christmas.
How cool is that ?!!?
Tomorrow morning I will go outside and start a
very reliable car (Jeep) and go to work at a job
where it does not appear that I am in
any immediate danger of losing. AND, even if I did,
I have the experience and abilities to continue working either on
my own or be hired on elsewhere at or above my current wage.
My health is outstanding,
and my sense of humor continues to be FANTASTIC.
(not a word out of the peanut gallery :p)
There is a huge connection between those two, by the way.

SO... I think I'll end my little thought of the day
by repeating a question a customer asked me today
after I had my lunchtime visit at the bank.

"How are you doing today ?"
I looked up, looked back at him and answered:
"Well, all things considered - pretty darn good."

It's when we don't consider the "all things"
that we may have a different answer...

> **What is the "handicap" in your life**
> **that keeps you from achieving your dreams -**
> **...and is it worth hanging onto ?**

Let Me Hear Your Song

I'm at the Salvation Army thrift store
standing in line to purchase a small dresser
I'd found to help organize what is my clothing chaos.

And I see him.
If one were to judge him by appearance, you might say
that he had run out of luck long ago and spent much time
amongst the out of work and possibly even the homeless.
So it was a bit odd to see him walk over to the somewhat
dilapidated looking piano that was sitting by the door,
just begging for a nice place to call Home.
He approached the still and silent piano slowly, touching
the old wood as if touching the hand of a fine elderly Lady.
Then he sat down on the well worn bench, which gave
a small creak and sigh of pleasure for the attention.

The sound of keys a bit out of tune began to ring out quietly
at first, as if afraid of what he might or might not hear.
He looked furtively around him, perhaps wondering if
someone might at any moment tell him to stop.
Tenderly and gingerly at first, considerate of
the aged keys, his tune began to breathe.

I caught a surprised smile cross the faces of a few around
me as what started out as shy hands began moving
across the keys with an experience well hidden
beneath the baggy coat and worn sleeves.
It was beautiful how quickly the fires of passion
overcame any fear, inhibition, and trepidation.

His fingers floated freely now across the keyboard, oblivious to
all but the music in his soul that would not be denied this moment.
It was magnificent as it was moving, and it seemed
magically surreal that it was happening before my eyes.

When at last the piece released, and the final notes satisfied,
his eyes closed for a moment and all around him was still.
He quietly closed the lid, his brief ebony and ivory affair over,
and melted back into the midst of his unsuspecting audience.

I paid for the furnishing that was being given a second chance,
and thought about this miracle of music that had just transpired.

How often do we pursue our passions?
In what moments do we cast off our inhibitions
and reservations to finally face and embrace
the song we so often stifle in our heart?

Why do we choose to play the practical
and follow the sensible and safe?

Time after time we are timid
with the dreams we hold within
and never allow them to blossom
or become the star of our Show.

I do not want to wait until my best years are gone
to finally play my part and sing my song.

Stop the noise around you
and face the silence.

Finally hear those shut out voices;
the pleas of your heart & soul
that yearn to be set free – and
follow the dreams you find there.

The world awaits your arrival…

YOU are the lead in this play of Life;
YOU are the conductor and orchestrator.
Act like it.
Stop waiting to see what comes next.
Stop trying to get the lines just right.
***Do not allow the curtain to close before
you realize this was no dress rehearsal.***

There is nothing of tangible significance
that separates the most successful from
the most desperate; from those who
have what they desire and those who
are still just hoping and wishing.

Stop wishing on a star;
realize **YOU ARE THE STAR** .

I want to see you shine – Let us hear your song!

The world is your audience. The admission has been paid.
We await the performance of your Life that IS your Life.

You will be brilliant, my friend.

Of that I have no doubt…

Memories In The making;
Choose wisely...

OK Gang -

As usual I don't know how this is going to go.

But I do know that I'm going to say some things

I've never shared with anyone in my Life...

Last weekend I was taking my son home

(a recent addition to the world of 4yr olds)

and out of the blue he said; "I sure have fun with you, Dad".

I beamed & my heart leapt, then he said;

"we get to go fishing, play XBox, and go to the park..."

(Earlier he had experienced his first fishing expedition)

Over the past year I've struggled with whether or not

we were growing apart. There had even been times I felt it

would be better if I wasn't in his life at all - that the shuffling back

& forth between parents was just tearing him apart emotionally.

I know it crushed me, and many times I'd drive away

in tears pounding the steering wheel... It's been hard.

I held his mother's hand while he was born;

it was an indescribable experience.

From that day forward my son and I literally

spent every day together for nearly two years.

We were inseparable.

Then his mother and I parted ways.

It sounds trite to say that since then time and circumstances

have changed; yet you all have your own versions of things

in your life that have brought you to where you are today.

So for now I'll keep this one to myself ;)

My point is:

Why not hold on to the most precious memory

of those who have been and are in our lives ?

And just as I have asked myself that question over

and over for the past 2 days; why not ask it of yourself.

Don't just casually do it now,

then go about your life "business as usual".

Let that question really set in.

Now the other side of that question is;

What memory are you holding on to ?

When you look at those people who have come into your Life -

regardless of where they are now, How do you remember them ?

There are those who have hurt me more deeply than I could

ever put into words. There are those who have betrayed me,

cheated me, lied to me, stolen from me... The list goes on.

Most of my life I've collected these "pictures of persecution"

and held on to my resentment of those responsible

as if it were a trophy; a martyr's reward.

So now the phrase "throw the baby out with the bathwater"

comes to mind. Not sure where that phrase came from,

but what it's telling me is that I've let a great many people

out of my life because of something they've done.

Now the phrase "Forgive and forget" comes to mind.

I don't know that I'm ready for that, to be honest.

I'm no saint - and it's far easier said than done.

And yet... I'm ready to find the rose

where previously I've seen only thorns.

Instead of bitterness;

I can see someone who gave me a beautiful son.

In place of a broken heart;

savoring home cooked pasta while watching a movie –

and falling asleep in each other's arms - smiling...

Rather than brood over business failures;

recall the victory of my first paying client ;)

Now, does this mean that I'm going to disregard the past

and pretend everything is "OK" ? Ahhhh... No.

I refer you back to my earlier statement; I am not a saint.

I'm also smart enough to learn from experience,

and strong enough to act on it.

My goal is not to welcome these people back -

my "Pollyanna" days are long gone, and

I have many people to thank for this ;)

It is best some people remain out of our lives,

and I accept that this may not go over well with everyone.

Still, come on - there's a reason they're gone !

I just think life would be happier if every time

we thought of someone or were

reminded of someone on our "bad" list -

it wouldn't stress us out, make us angry

or otherwise upset our current world.

So I'm going to choose a bit differently
what I remember most about you.
I was going to say "people" instead of "you",

There are many people who have walked in and out of my Life;
most of them will never know what I've just shared with you.
So listen, please - whether you know me or not;
I hope our experience right now is one you can
take away with you and remember with a smile.
And if there's someone who you're thinking of
at this very moment and you're holding a memory
of them that's a dark cloud for you – and so far
maybe you can't forgive, maybe you can't forget...
But pick a cherished memory to represent them,
move beyond that darkness,
and get on with your Life.
I am reminded now, as I am so often
of these words from Helen Keller;

"Keep your face to the sunshine,
and you cannot see the shadows."

Moments Like These

There are many reasons for me to smile today,
but the one that put the biggest smile on my face
is one that was unplanned & unexpected.
I was on the way to my brother's house with a very chatty
4 year old (hereto referred to as "son").
After about 4 minutes of chatter, there was silence.
Realizing that my last 3 random conversations were with
a now sleeping boy, I was glad he was finally resting.
After a long hard day of fun & play AND a new bicycle
AND a very exciting Easter egg hunt he was
getting grumpy & really really needed a nap !

So I arrived at my brothers, carried the still zonked
heir of my throne to the door... and it was locked. Ugh.
I hadn't exactly planned the timing of my visit - my bad :p
Fortunately I had a key, so I went in, took 2 pairs of shoes off
and laid down with my son on the couch. My intention was
to get him settled in so he could nap. But you know...
I looked at him - this little boy who I could once carry in the
crook of my arm; his little hand was curled just so on my chest.
His lips were in the shape of a smile - the smile brought on
by a deep slumber filled with a peace known only by angels..
and a small sleeping child ;) I could hear his breathing,
interrupted by an occasional snore.
So I laid there for a while - relishing
the quiet serenity of the moment.
I felt he could hear my own breathing,
along with my heartbeat - and it made me recall
the many naps we'd had together when he was a baby.
How I miss those times. How I miss him.

He has recently moved away - farther than ever before,
and even though it is only distance, I fear there may be
a time where he and I become out of touch...
I suppose that's every parents worry, though.
They grow up so fast !
Someday I won't hear those words "Pick me up, Daddy"...
chuckle...
It's already changed to "pick me up, Dad" or just "pick me up" !
So I whisper "Hold my neck", and he does - and I scoop him up...

I was going to write this originally to share
how much happiness and contentment I felt
with my son sleeping on my chest...
and now I realize that any time I recall these moments
I am the happiest I have ever been in my Life.
All in all, no matter how much they grow up
they will always be our little Angels.
May we never forget that.

Thank you for yet another priceless moment, son...

I love you.

~Dad

My Hero For The Day

I'm standing in a store and this guy comes in and he's looking
for something. I don't even know what it was or if he found it,
but before he left has asked of everyone present:
"Do you know anyone with a house for rent?"
Those present did not, and then he asked;
"Do you have any newspapers here?"
He was informed they did not sell newspapers there.
"Do any of you have any - did you bring one in with you?"
No one did, but I did suggest he stop at the nearest Starbucks
just up the road because I was fairly sure that they would have
a few that had been left there by customers who like to read
their paper over coffee. As he was leaving, I heard him say:
"Living in a Winnebago with 5 people kind of sucks."
And, I can't believe I said this, but I looked at him, smiled,
and said; "I'll bet you could leave off the "kind of" !
His eyes met mine, and I could tell he knew I felt his pain…
Little did he know that he had inspired me!
To me, this was yet another example of living a life less ordinary
moving towards extraordinary. It is a reminder to stop wondering
what might and start making wonderful things happen.

So let's bring this into your World.
~   What if you got what you asked for?
And speaking of asking, may I ask what it is that
you think is "OK" or "appropriate" to ask others -
and then will you tell me why?
Let that roll around your head for a bit.
If you follow this sidetrack, you may just discover something
as revealing as it is limiting about yourself regarding
the things you will ask for – and what you won't.

Years ago I was involved in a seminar in which part
of one assignment was to come up with things that
were unreasonable and beyond comfort - especially
in the area of asking others. It was actually this type
of thinking and acting that was responsible for my
being sponsored in the first 10K race I ever ran !
I even ended up with a little extra $$$:)
One of the biggest things I got out of this experience
was discovering in a very real and Life altering way
that people want to help people. They really do.
Think back to a time when you were able to reach out and
help someone. Felt good, didn't it ? To be able to contribute to
the Life of another and make a difference holds a reward all its own.
(Note: Stop stealing this from people who want to help!)

Yet most people have been brought up to think that there
is great pride in being able to do everything yourself –
that it means you are a better person if you can "Do it all."
However, history shows us time after time that those who
enlist the support and assistance of others in their endeavors
have accomplished and achieved the most. Those who go
beyond the "normal" and "acceptable" and reach instead
for what is or may be possible - they are rewarded for
that which they pursue; not what they continually pass up
or believe may be "too much to ask" or "unreasonable".
All in all, any time I have practiced this in earnest -
and done so with hope, yet without attachment to any
set response; I have been amazed with the things
that have come as a result of simply asking.

So let's pretend there is no limit to what we can ask of Life
and those who share it with us. And here's a little secret -
about that thing I asked you to let roll around in your head?
Let's imagine that you're worth it and that you deserve it.

So I'm going to say something I've said time and time again
in hopes it sinks in. In this Life – this one life we have to live -
most of us give up and in too soon and play small.
We don't ask for more, and we expect so much less.

Practice living a bold and amazing life;
request of this World and we who live in it
the means with which to build your dreams.

If we never ask, we'll never get:
and if we shoot for the stars - we might just get the moon…

NOW would be a good time to be completely excited
at the possibilities and opportunities that await you.
Speaking of waiting - What are YOU waiting for?!?!?

No More Excuses!

I'm sitting here procrastinating something
that many people actually enjoy.
Singing; more specifically karaoke style.
I located a place in Vancouver that has Karaoke Night,
called them and was informed that their karaoke begins at 9pm.
It is 9:23 and here I sit typing you !
This isn't to say that it's your fault,
but it sure is working to keep me from going ;)
Sigh.
Doesn't that just work, though ?
The excuse, that is; it's working very well.
So I was going to say that I find singing in front of people
a terrifying experience, but what's really fascinating me now is
how well this excuse is working - this little tangent, sidetrack, etc.
It's taken up 5 minutes so far.
(9:28)
It reminds me of something I heard years ago.
A friend of mine - very successful in business,
shared that he once asked his son to do something.
Okay, so now I can't recall the exact dialog - but in a
nutshell the excuse was made that he was making soup.
The point of the story was that
ANY excuse will work if you use it.
(It is 9:41)

Now, I could go on and on in my life where I've let excuses,
reasons, etc. keep me from doing things.
But of course it's waaaay easier pointing the fingers at YOU.
So, while we're pointing, what excuse have you used lately ?

Okay, that's too broad a subject. I'll pick one for you.

How about an area of your life that you are uncomfortable with.

Maybe you're afraid to try something (karaoke? skydiving??).

Perhaps you want to say something to someone,

but aren't sure how they'll take it.

Maybe your work came in 2nd place next to Hell...

and yet you're still working there

What about... feelings for another ?

Hey - you pick, you know what they are and you know

that you've got plenty to pick from !

How's the soup ?

How has what you've picked to be the reason you

are not living the life you want treating you these days ?

Ouch.

Remember - I'm still pointing at you,

so 3 fingers are pointing back at me.

(9:51)

My friend also said this; It's easier not to.

It's easier NOT to do something than to do something,

and most people are "lazy" in their lives and reactive

instead of proactive - and it doesn't matter how "busy" you are.

It's easier not to look for another job.

It's easier to put off making a phone call.

It's easier not sharing your feelings.

It's easier to give up on love...

But those things that are supposedly easier

make a much harder Life in the long run;

and a watered down, bland life at that.

Don't you think it's time to wake up ?

(10:00)

((Finger still pointed at you - 3 at me))

Stop finding reasons why you can't,
excuses why you don't
- and find a purpose
that will push you beyond.

Tonight I'm taking you with me to a place I've never been
doing something that is the most uncomfortable thing I know of.

Don't chicken out on me, OK ?
Pick your own battle, challenge, demon
- and face it, embrace it; beat it.

It's 10:07 right now,
and I'm out the door at 10:10.
Promise.
No more excuses ;)

Nothing To Lose,
and Everything To Gain.

Can you deal with it ?

Chances are if you tell 5 people about something you want,
one of those people can bring you closer to getting it -
either directly or knowing someone else that can.

So what I would like to do is help you get one step closer.
Let's really take a look at this - I'm not writing this as some
observation or thought provoking idea to tuck away & forget.

Brass tacks gang - seriously !

You do not know everyone that I know,
just as I do not know everyone you know.
AND when it comes to the people you and I know -
we don't know everyone or everything they know !!!

Now before we both get dizzy here,
the only thing to keep in mind is this:
You don't know what you don't know,
and you don't know who you don't know.
So you don't know where and from whom
help may come, nor is it likely you'll even
know what it will look like.
Got it ? Good :)

Now, if you're serious about this -
you tell me something that you want that til now
has just seemed out of reach, or some challenge
or problem in your Life that you cannot overcome.

At some point I should mention this:
If we actually find solutions to our problems and
eliminate the roadblocks to our success and what we want;
we will run out of excuses, and have only ourselves to blame.

Whereas...
If we continue to avoid taking real and affirmative action,
we can always talk about our dreams, goals and aspirations
to gain the attention - without really having to work for them.

I'm just throwing that out there for those who talk the talk
but will not walk the walk when it comes to changing their Life.
(You're not alone - my own life is peppered with such things)

All right - for those of you left:
this could be the most rewarding experience of your Life.
Find 5 people and share with them what it is you want.
Do it in a way that they know beyond a shadow of a doubt
that you intend on getting it, and be crystal clear in your intent.
Convey it believing that they can and will move within their
own lives and connect with others who will be a part of it.

Expect a miracle, and act accordingly...

Now Is A Lucky Time For You -
Take A Chance !

I'm looking down at my keyboard and there is a fortune
sitting there that I retrieved from my wallet / pocket filing cabinet.
(No, it did not come with the wallet - it came inside a fortune cookie)

" NOW IS A LUCKY TIME FOR YOU - TAKE A CHANCE "

Well first off, let's get one thing straight.
NOW IS A LUCKY TIME. Period. Got that ?
Tomorrow - sketchy.
Yesterday - possibly,
but only when it was NOW.

So, given that NOW is indeed a lucky time -
what are you waiting for ? Take a chance !

Moving too fast ? Well, let's go slower.
Why don't you write this down and
tape it to your bathroom mirror.

" NOW IS A LUCKY TIME FOR YOU - TAKE A CHANCE "

(OK, I just wrote it on the mirror with a dry erase marker)
((Seriously - I did. Orange.))
Tomorrow morning when you drag yourself out of bed
and make your way into the bathroom - look in the mirror.
Read those words.
Now, look back at your reflection in the mirror.

Read the words again.
Now, I know it's early – but what if
you approached the day with this mindset ?

You see, most days we typically spend the majority of
our time bouncing around in our "boxes" of familiarity.
Taking a chance operates outside of what we "know"
the outcome of. It's unfamiliar, and most of the time
we'll shy away from the unknown.

Ah, but knowing NOW is a lucky time -
I'm thinking it's time to stirs things up a bit.
Reminds me of a fortune cookie I had way back:
"Take the chance while you still have the choice"
* Note to self - "Take a chance" does not mean be reckless - FYI...

So I'm curious what will you find to tackle,
given that now is a lucky time for you.

What will you try, Lucky?

Now Is The Time To Break The Chains...

Years ago I read a quote that, at the time
did not have the same impact and meaning
for me as it does today in my Life,
and I had all but forgotten about it until
earlier this week when it was sent to me.

So... before you read it, though - a few thoughts.
First of all - I think you and I are afraid that
we aren't good enough or "adequate" enough
on some level or some area of our lives.
And for the most part we either ignore avoid
those things where we feel inadequate about, or
we tackle them head on until they become a strength.

============================

" Attack that which you fear
and the death of fear is certain. "

" Do that which you fear the most
   and it will one day become
   your greatest strength. "

============================

Yet, there is something deeper and more powerful;
a truth that most only catch a glimpse of before
quickly dismissing it as an impossibility.
As a matter of fact, If you were to grasp and embrace this,
you wouldn't spend your time on any of those petty fears
and so called inadequacies that you make up.

Stepping further -
up to this point you have done much
to cover up, disguise and deny this truth.

So much so that no matter what I say here,
and despite my efforts to convey and reveal it -
I suspect that your reactions will be to smile,
then smirk, and finally scoff at the mere notion.

So read this.
And do me a favor.
Read beyond the words.
Whether you are agnostic, religious, atheist -
put your beliefs on hold right now & don't
let them be a hang up or hindrance to you.
Don't let your faith or lack thereof
be a feather in your cap for failure.

OK. I think that's it.
Now, let this sink in:

"Our deepest fear is not that we are inadequate.
Our deepest fear is that we are powerful beyond measure.
It is our light, not our darkness, that most frightens us.
We ask ourselves, who am I to be brilliant, gorgeous,
talented, and fabulous? Actually, who are you not to be?
You are a child of God.
Your playing small doesn't serve the world.

There's nothing enlightened about shrinking so that
other people won't feel insecure around you.
We are all meant to shine, as children do.
We are born to make manifest the glory of God that is within us.
It's not just in some of us, it's in everyone.
And as we let our own light shine, we unconsciously
give other people permission to do the same.
As we are liberated from our own fear,
our presence automatically liberates others."

~ Marianne Williamson

OK, now for those of you who simply skimmed this -
consider that there are other areas of your life as well
where your rush to find what you're looking for
prevents you from seeing what there is to find.

Because here's the deal:
there is a lot that could be done to
make this world a better place to live.
And I happen to think that you are the solution.
Not a politician, nor any "package" or clever slogan.
No head of a church or chairman of any board.
You need to get - really grasp and embrace -
that you are a force to be reckoned with in your world,
and that you are the change that will
make a difference to the world.

The world around you as you know it
exists because you have allowed it to be.
By what you've done, or not done and allowed to occur,
you are living a life of your own creation –
not circumstance or chance.
And as you wake up and become the cause
of how the world around you evolves and revolves -
those around you will stir from their own self induced slumber.
When majoring in the minors becomes a thing of the past
and playing small is no longer part of your game plan;
people will see that and want to be a part of it.
They will join you in the transformation
of both your Life and theirs.

Now is the time to break the chains...

Out Of Sight (Out Of Mind)

While I was walking down the aisle at a store some
time ago, a rather attractive young lady looked at me,
smiled, and looked away. Well, I thought that was
pretty cool - a nice boost to my ego :)
Of course, I was wearing my lucky sweater.
* I've nicknamed it my lucky sweater because it is
my favorite, lightweight & incredibly comfortable.
It is brown in color and those of you who know me or
have met me have probably seen it by now UNLESS
you met me on a hot day and haven't seen me since.
I will more than likely pass this sacred sweater down
to my son when he is 18, who will be gracious in
its acceptance and either hide it away in his closet
or donate it to Goodwill...

Meanwhile, back at the ranch... or in this case store.
A little while later, a couple of girls smiled at me &
sort of giggled after I had passed.
Flirtatious vixens - probably acting all kinds of silly
when a handsome young lad as myself is near.
My, I was starting to feel like quite the stud!
Even some dude gave me the nod - like I was all
kinds of cool. On the way home I was feeling about
6' 4" and contemplating when I would start booking
my GQ photo shoot and what agency to represent me.

Brace yourselves;
everything is about to come crashing down.

I went into the bathroom after I got home,
looked in the mirror and saw the huge stain of
taco sauce down the left side of my mouth... face.

And it wasn't just your average dark red taco sauce.
This stuff was a very light orange-pinkish color.
Very very tasty and incredibly messy.

What I learned, aside from remembering to
Wipe that delicious taco sauce off my face
(or should I say what I was reminded of) is

There are things about us that we do not see -
that we do not know.

STOP !

Savor that point.

       There are things about us
           that we do not see -
               that we do not know.

There are things about us that
we do not see - that we do not know.

Now, give me an example.
I'll wait.

Make it a good one...

I'm patient.

Seriously - I can wait :)

And you know,
even a small example would be OK...

So... I'm not trying to pressure you or anything,

but I would like to, you know - get to the point...

tonight

sometime...

I just need an example any example, OK ?
OOOoooookay then

- I'm just going to finish this up here while you're thinking.
If you are still thinking & haven't come up with an example,
that is exactly my point.
If you did manage to find an example - think again.
Tell me something about yourself that you do not know
something about yourself that you do not see.

You can't, because you don't know it's there.

(Or as a very wealthy person once said -

"you don't know what you don't know")

BUT JUST BECAUSE YOU CAN'T SEE IT

OR DON'T KNOW ABOUT IT

DOESN'T MEAN IT'S NOT THERE.

It doesn't mean that it's not having an effect on your Life

and on those around you. Quite the contrary:

All too often it's the things

that we are not aware of

that determine and dictate so much

of what we do and do not do.

With that in mind, there is a very good chance

all your efforts thus far are done to affect and have

an effect only on that which you are aware of and see.

You and I are all aware of the things we do know and

suspect are causing and creating both our victories

and our failures; yet when we hit a wall and find ourselves

unable to move forward - there are things of which we are

not aware, things that we are blind to seeing and knowing,

that are continually tripping us up and making us fall and fail...

Realizing this is the first step

to seeing what you are looking for and finding it...

Saving It For The Trip Back

Shortly after we sat down on the plane
I could feel it, and I knew I had about a minute before my
nice white shirt would soon be splattered red. Nosebleed.
Great. I didn't plan for that. No napkins, no tissue... No time.
So I did what any McGiver-like wanna be would do in my situation.
I took my right sock off and used it to stem the flow of blood !
As near as I could tell, I don't think anyone even noticed.
Of course, before the plane landed, I took my left sock off to match :)

As with most things that bounce around in my head and
make connections that make my closest friends just shake
their heads and smile, I thought of the movie "Gattaca".
But of course, you too, right ??? Of course !
You see, the main character in the movie had a few health issues -
challenges that, for the dreams and goals that he had for his Life
would have prevented him from reaching them.
That is... if he chose only to look at his circumstances and situation.

I would encourage you to watch the movie some time,
as for me at least it showed me countless examples of
how determination, perseverance, and willpower overcame
what many - MOST people would deem the impossible.

You see, most people allow excuses & reasons
to become a "truth" as to what we can or cannot do,
letting it rule both our attitudes and our actions in Life.

I say "we" not only because I am a "people", but because I'm
as guilty as any in allowing myself to hold onto the excuses
and what I perceive to be very real and valid "reasons"
(of course they are, or they wouldn't work !) that
hold and hinder me from reaching my own stars.

Oh, I know at times I've "changed my mind" on some goals, or
decided to "take a different course" in other pursuits and passions.
Instead of shooting for the stars, we aim instead at the moon, right?
Well, giving up has many different names and shows up
in many ways. And no one likes to say they gave up...
especially to themselves. Let's just be honest about that.

So real quick let me run down
something that I hope hits home with you.
Bear with me here as I give you the short version.
THIS IS WORTH IT !

There were once 2 brothers.
The younger brother (Anton) had excellent health,
while the older brother (Vincent) had health challenges.
When they were kids, they would swim out to sea
and whoever went furthest before turning back won.
Victory was always the younger, stronger brother's.
UNTIL one day... Not only does he swim further,
but he ends up saving his brother from drowning.
Years later, the answer as told from
the weaker brother to the stronger:
"You wanna know how I did it?
This is how I did it Anton.
I never saved anything for the swim back..."

    "I never saved anything for the swim back".

208

I see this in numerous situations, both professional and personal.
For example, those who don't quite commit themselves
fully into their relationships - keeping one foot just ever
so slightly in the doorway so they can run (again).
I see it from the entrepreneur who has just one too many setbacks,
who goes back to a 9 to 5 job - and turns their back to their dream.

In so many scenarios and situations,
people holding back from going all out -
always trying to save enough for the "swim back";
never truly committing themselves and giving it their all.

So, do you mind if I ask -
When you finally gave up and gave in;
Why did you? Now, normally I'd let you off the hook
with whatever you tell me was your excuse / reason.
After all, it was good enough for you !

But... not so much tonight.
Unless you've had your head in the sand until reading this,
you know by now that I know you're capable of far more.

What is
the bottom line reason for giving up?
Or are you afraid that
your all isn't enough...
and then what?

Wouldn't that mean you failed?

Wouldn't it mean you aren't good enough?
If you put your word behind your endeavor and say
"This is what I am doing
and this is where I am going -
I will not be deterred,
and though I may falter I will not fail
because I will not quit: I will never give up."

What would it mean... if you did give up?

Does it give you goosebumps to think what might happen
if you truly did give your all into... Well, in anything?

Now - give me some credit here and humor me.
If you tell me you tried levitating before and no matter what,
it didn't happen. Hold up. First, I'd say you're doing it wrong,
and second I'd ask you to stop trying to squirm your way out
of discovering some very deep rooted "truths" about yourself.

You know that saying that goes: "The Truth shall set you free" ?
Well, I don't recall hearing the other half: that it would probably
scare the living you know what out of you, too !

I'm going to cut this short for now, but something to think about.
Looking back over your Life - reviewing the many things that
you've given up on (don't get all hung up on those words, OK?)
can you honestly truthfully and 100% look yourself in eye
(use a mirror) and say that you did everything you could to
make it happen - that you poured yourself 100% completely
into it and there was nothing else you could do -
nothing else that could be done?

If you answered "No" –
I thank you for your honest insight.
And... if you answered "Yes" - try putting aside
your belief in the reasons, excuses and justifications
that gave you permission to quit.
That may be the toughest part,
but also the most rewarding and revealing.

You know, I never really sat down and pondered
what it is that I'd like written on my tombstone,
but it seems like these words would do me proud;

"I never saved anything for the swim back"

I've got a long way to go...
How are you doing?

Scraps of Paper

If any of you have seen my wallet,
you will have noticed that it is rather "fat".
As much as I would like it to be full of cash,
it's actually full of scraps of paper.
A piece of napkin, a post-it note, gas receipt, etc.
On each is written a reminder of something.
Let's just take a look now :)

A piece of an orange post-it that says
"A good day to let it go...
What are you holding onto
that you should let go? "

Along the side it says "moments".

Here's a green Post-it that says
"You may not be able to change the World -
but you might influence someone who can..."

Here's another green post-it cut in half
      "Do you prioritize
         the immediate & pressing
            or the important ?"

And another piece of green post-it says
"We seem to practice our morality
when it serves us / is convenient"

And there you have it –
a few of the things that I need to tell you,
and I write these notes because I don't want to forget.
But the note I really need to write is "WRITE !!!"
These scraps of paper aren't doing either of us
any good hiding out in my wallet, and I have
143,170 reasons to create and allow them
to become something that might make
a difference to someone somewhere…

It's the least I can do.

Sometimes You Hear Back...

Back in my early days when I was a budding entrepreneur,
I was on a business trip and stopped at a Shari's restaurant
as I was passing through the town of Tacoma, WA.
(Shari's is my favorite 24hr place to hang when I want to think,
write, and think some more) .
I don't recall much about the visit itself, but I do remember
there was something I found special about the server.
Now, I used to do something that I don't do much anymore,
and that is leave notes. This particular night I left a note
expressing not only my appreciation of the service,
but a few things I saw & appreciated about her.
I also ended it with my usual little poem I wrote in high school;

"Go after what you want in Life
don't let it pass you by
Never give up and be caught in strife
you can do anything if you try."

I left my note (written on a napkin),
dropped my tip, and drove home.
Fast forward. It's nearly a year later and I'm meeting up
with an old friend I hadn't seen in a couple of years
who had moved to Kelso, WA. (I was living in Bremerton)
and we decided to meet at a Shari's off the highway
in Tacoma because it was easy for us to find.
How she recognized me I'll never know
- but the same waitress I had left the note for came over
to the table. She told me she remembered me, and
said that she wanted to thank me for the note - sharing
that she still had it tacked to the mirror in her room.

The look in her eyes held more appreciation than words ever could.
I've had many a rolled eye my way for leaving notes...
Come to think of it, people roll their eyes at a lot of things I do ;)
But in that moment... it was worth it - and nothing else mattered.

You and I probably do a lot of things for other people
- and more often than not we don't let them know it.
It's just how we are. We walk quietly into the sunset with a smile,
wondering if they'll ever figure it out
- and not caring that they ever do...
You walk this Life with a Midas touch;
leaving others you encounter a little richer.

And sometimes, just sometimes

                        you hear back...

~ dedicated to those
            who have reached out to me
            when I was unreachable;
            touched me
            when I was untouchable
            and lifted me
            when I had no desire to rise...

Sticks and Stones
May Break My Bones,
But What's Really Holding Us Back ?

I don't know the technical name of the device -
but you know those devices at the airport that you can walk
through and it will show all of the weapons of mass destruction
that one might be carrying on them - like, fingernail nail clippers?
Yeah, that one.

So I'm sitting here thinking that if Paul McCartney walked through
one of those, would the guy looking at the monitor know it was him?
(Don't ask - I heard a lot of Beatles tunes earlier today)
Do you think if Julia Roberts walked through that device, followed
by Oprah Winfrey, that either of them would look much different
than any other woman who walked through that day?
Just as the skeletal structure of our current president would appear
no more special than that of my own, the basic framework of people
is the same. Similarly, as well, the bodies that hang on that frame.
(though depending on lifestyle choices may visually differ).

Matter-of-fact, if you were to bury the neighbor next door
alongside the president of the United States and dig the
bodies up 100 years from now there would be nothing
there to distinguish the 'prince' from the pauper.

So what's the difference ?
This is one of the things that constantly...
Well, at the same time it fascinates me - it also infuriates me.
Now - don't worry if you think I'm talking about you. I am.
Just as I can look in the mirror and see
the cause and the cure of my own limitations.

Here's a thought.

If you've ever met anyone who you would deem "successful",
there are certain ACTIONS they took that got them there.

You know what ?

In the past I would often use the excuse of what "they" had that
I didn't have as a reason why I wasn't achieving how I wanted.

What I mean is, I would look at their situation,
and the things that I lacked I made to be one of
the big reasons they were succeeding and I wasn't.

They had (insert something I didn't here) and
therefore they could succeed & I couldn't.

See ?

It is possibly one of THE greatest excuses that people have
come up with so far as a reason to fail or "settle for" less.

We all come into this world
with nothing but bones & flesh.

Everything else we achieve
or acquire throughout Life.

We all start from nothing;
and can all rise to anything.

Now,

whether you're nineteen or ninety -
it's never too early or late to start from
the same nothing we were all born with.

Anything up to this point
you will choose to either look at
as a boost to your success or as
further baggage to hold you back.

You and me both. :)

Take A Few Minutes

I received this very short, but very impacting letter today from
the mother of my son. It probably took less than 2 minutes
from start to finish to write, but you know... I'll never forget it.

" I just wanted you to know that you are
the closest man I have ever had to me,
and I appreciate you so much.

I don't know what I would have done
if I didn't let someone get to know me
as much as you do.

I know it is not your birthday,
but thank you for being born...

     love,
         me :) "

Take a few minutes
to tell someone how you feel about them...

You may never know the impact
        you can have on another,
    or the impact
   it could have
on you...

Take The Chance While
You Still Have The Choice...

My son asked me for a fortune cookie today,
and though I told him they were stale and unsavory,
he wanted one anyway. It was worth it, because
when he opened it up, this jewel was prize within:

" Take the chance while you still have the choice. "

Yesterday I had written a few phrases down on a
Post-It note and stuck it in my wallet,
adding to my ever growing collection.
"What if..." "What might have been?" "If only..."

So, the timing of this fortune cookie = perfect.
Because really....
How many times have you asked yourself
any number of questions like that ?
What if I had stayed in Indiana
instead of moving to the Northwest?
If only I'd said "no" to "Let's do something really fun".
What might have been...

There are so many things that present themselves to us;
and all of them are opportunities - yet are they opportunities
we are aware of, or do they seem more like a challenge ?
And by the way, most opportunities do meet us
in the form of a challenge, so if you find yourself
seriously lacking in the "opportunity" department -
take a closer look at the challenges that face you every day.
F.Y.I. :)

Because here's the not so pretty part of an opportunity:
it can disappear as quickly as it arrived -
and we may never be able to get it back.

" Take the chance while you still have the choice. "

Notice the first word is "Take", which is an action word.
Also notice that the last word is "Choice"
meaning that it's in your hands.

We can never know how different our lives would be
if only we had made different decisions,
choices and actions in our past.
It's fun to guess & imagine sometimes,
and at other times it's a very tearful thought.

What I can tell you is that although we cannot change the past,
we can learn from it and better steer the course of our future.

Take a good look at the moments that come and go -
look for the ingredients that would propel you forward
to more of the Life you wish to be a part of.
And pay special attention to the challenges
and obstacles that come your way,
and how you act and react to them.

Are you saying "no" when you really don't know ?

Because I want your Life to be filled with
a lot more "I'm glad I did" memories
than "If only I'd..." regrets.

The Dance

Several years ago a coworker gave me a cassette
tape that was a compilation of mostly country music.
It was meant to be a joke, because everyone knew
I couldn't stand country music. Not knowing what was
on the tape, I played it. I'd listen to a few seconds of one,
fast forward to the next, etc. Ugh... But one caught my attention
because it started out with a piano intro - and I love the piano.
How deceptive ! It was an OK song, but it was still COUNTRY,
so I recorded the beginning and the end of it over and over
on both sides of the tape, leaving out all but the piano !
Yet I made the mistake of listening to it - really listening to it.

So here it is - "The Dance", by Garth Brooks:

"Looking back on the memory of
The dance we shared beneath the stars above
For a moment all the world was right
How could I have known you'd ever say goodbye

And now I'm glad I didn't know
The way it all would end
the way it all would go
Our lives are better left to chance
I could have missed the pain
But I'd of had to miss the dance

Holding you I held everything
For a moment wasn't I the king
But if I'd only known how the king would fall
Hey who's to say you know I might have changed it all

221

And now I'm glad I didn't know
The way it all would end
the way it all would go
Our lives are better left to chance
I could have missed the pain
But I'd of had to miss the dance

Yes my life is better left to chance
I could have missed the pain
but I'd of had to miss the dance..."

That song opened up a respect for country music that
I had not allowed before, and now I hold country
music with appreciation rather than disdain.

So tell me this - when you read the lyrics to the song
 (you did, right?) what did you get out of it ?
It's many things to me.
It describes a past relationship;
In it I felt like a king, and she my Lady.
When it ended, I was devastated.
But looking back, the dance we had was worth it.
Never would I have experienced such an intensity
of love and passion - to know what that was like.
And even the deepest wounds heal in time.

There are so many things in our lives that we often wish
we could change. Yet if we did - what would we miss?

I'm reminded of a story heard years ago.

A woman, overcome with grief, was granted a wish.

She could have all of her memories washed away -

all of her sadness, pain and tragedies would be gone.

But when she realized that she would also lose her moments

of happiness, joys and triumph - she declined the granted wish.

You and I have been through things that at first we wish

we'd never been. Heck, we may never think otherwise!

And though it's easy to say that the bitter in our lives makes

the good all the more sweet, it is so hard to swallow that pill.

Still, experience has taught me and brought me many things

that if it were not through adversity, I would not have "danced"

with so much joy in this Life and held the happiness I have.

And once again, as it is with so much I try to share with you

- what I've said has hit me the hardest, and on this day

I can say that I am thankful for what I have received

- no matter what it might look like...

The Earth Was Always Round

One of the things that holds us back the most
is not believing or accepting those things
that we do not agree with or view as true.

So I ask you -
How was the world transformed when
Columbus revealed the Earth was round?
How did the Wright brothers revolutionize the world of travel and
transportation when they proved flight for mankind was possible?

Most of the world did not see it or believe it
prior to its "discovery" - still it was true.
Similarly, the World is round whether or not
Columbus ever discovered it to be so, just as
a billion people believing it was flat
did not make it less round.

Yet those discoveries around you and I
will not impact our lives as much as
those things hidden within us.

If you were shown those tendencies and traits about yourself
that continually thwart your progress to living the life you desire -
What would you do... if you didn't believe it?

Those habits that hinder you and hold you back -
what if you continued to ignore them as cause
for so much of what you claim you do not want?

You'd never soar to the heights you're capable of,
nor go as far as your dreams would carry you
for fear of falling off the edge...

So what do YOU believe holds you back?
Do you know?
If you do know, what are you doing about it?

Will you be open to the notion that
what you believe is stopping you
may be something other than
what you see and know?

It could be the most
important conversation,
resulting in the most amazing
realizations and revelations,
that you will ever have...

The Nail...

It's hard to know where to begin.
Then again, it usually is - and that's the very reason
I'm stopped so many times from writing you.
So much to say - and so much Life getting in the way...
If it weren't for that nail, tonight would be just another
missed opportunity to talk with you.

You see, there was an old hound dog at the neighbor's house, and
one day a friend came by who hadn't seen him for quite some time.
While they talked about the good ole days, the hound on the porch
would raise his head howl a few times, then put his head back down.
At first it didn't seem too unusual, but after a few more times of the
dog howling, the friend finally asked what the heck was wrong.
Turns out the old hound was laying on a nail - and it hurt!
So he asked why didn't the dog just get up off the nail & move.
"Well" he said "the nail doesn't hurt him THAT bad..."

You know, I've been taking a look at many things in my Life,
and it sure seems like I have a lot of complaints.
Oh, you'll never hear about most of them
- I tend to keep most of my gripes to myself.
Guess you could say I'm laying on a lot of "nails".
And yet... I don't get up & move. Crazy. CRAZY !
Is it that I'm so used to being uncomfortable, that now it's
easier to just put up with it than do what it takes to deal with it ?
Of course, I'm reminded daily of this as I observe
other people, and yes - sometimes even you.

Looking at it from the outside, it's almost funny;
we both "talk" about these nails as if that will help.

Which reminds me - ever notice that if it weren't for such talks some people wouldn't have much to talk about?
It's as if on some level there is a reward for telling others about the "nails" in our lives and how much they hurt us.
Try this little experiment. Find someone who is constantly complaining about something. Help them "fix" it and notice how quickly they find a new "thing" to complain about...

Ah, but that's not the direction I want to go...   Actually, the direction I want to go is the bed - because it's almost 2am :p
I could do the easier thing - the more comfortable thing, which would be to put this off and go to sleep.
So what if it's been bugging me for two weeks?
What's another night? Why not just lay on it a while longer.
It's just a nail...   "Howlllllllllll..."

So what you must know is that I just deleted a paragraph of really great examples of "nails" that I apparently like to lay on more than I am willing to move off of. I just figured some of you have some really great examples yourself. Matter-of-fact, a few of you have been my all too often reminders!
Yes, let's turn the mirror of examination around for you to see... You.
Why haven't you pursued that new job ?
You keep saying you're tired of how you're treated at work...
Why do you stay with that jerk - he treats you like garbage!
Didn't I hear you say that you were offered a scholarship
- and instead you still want to stock shelves at night... why?

Maybe what you really need is a longer nail.
That's not what I want - and that's not what I want for you.
But come on... **get off the nail!**
You have no idea how much it's really hurting you.

This Will Hurt Me More Than You

I had a tear in my eye tonight (well, to be honest, a few) after I
put my son to bed and we'd kissed each other goodnight.
I had almost made it to the door before I heard
his little voice say "I love you, Dad"

Looking back at the morning's events, I'd carried a heavy heart
throughout the day. Long story short, choices were made and
actions were taken that led to a few good whacks on his bee hind.
His tears were shed then. One of the things I shared with him,
as was told to me many times while growing up,
is that "It hurts me more than it does you".
I don't think I ever really "got" that back then.
As a parent, though – it's loud and clear.
It really does hurt us more.
And… on many levels.

If you're a parent, you've probably had those thoughts of
inadequacy, the questioning where you went wrong;
the fear that you're failing as a parent.
(How bad are you screwing your kid up?!?)
Where do you draw the line ? What battles do you pick ?
What are the boundaries ? How far should you give ?
Do you give in at all ? Is this worth it ?
So many doubts. So many times left saying; "What have I done ?"

This and so so very much more is what I took in
with me as I walked into his room tonight.
Did I deserve a hug ?
Would I get a kiss ?
Did he still… love me ?

Because beneath it all - that's what's really there;
THAT is what is underneath… so many things.
And so it was that our goodnight hug was a bit longer than usual,
and that we both squeezed one another a bit tighter.
Kisses exchanged with twinkling eyes.
My bid of "Goodnight, I love you" met
with only a "Goodnight" in return.

I was doing fine, I held it together. Almost to the door…
And then the music to my heart;

"I love you, Dad"

And I knew he meant it :)

ps:
to my son...
If one day you ever find this and read it - you will smile,
shake your head and say "You were right, Dad…"
And if you are reading it now, know that from the bottom of my heart
I have loved you before you took your first breath, and my love for you
has only grown greater since then. Nothing you have done,
nothing you do nor will do will ever diminish nor tarnish
the depth of my love for you. Always…
Always and every day I love you.

Love,

~ Dad

To My Son

I'm driving over to my brother's tonight and
I started to think of things that made me happy.
(you should try this sometime).

What prompted it was thinking how lucky I was
to have a son who for no apparent reason
will run over to me and kiss my leg
(that's as high as he can reach for now)
and give me a hug and a kiss.
No matter what I might be feeling prior to this event,
all time stops and every problem in the world melts away.

A little lump forms in my throat,
sometimes a tear in my eye;
and I'm overcome by love
both for him and from him.
For a moment it's as if the love of God
is reaching out through those little arms -
holding me; and holding me together.

I hope he never gets too "grown up" to stop giving
me those hugs, those kisses & "I love you Dad" s...

I love you, Son.

~Dad

What Are You Hoping Will Save You ?

The story has been told about a man who
was at home taking a nap, when suddenly
there was a frantic pounding on his front door.
Opening the door, a young boy hurriedly
informed him that a flood was coming and
that he needed to evacuate immediately.
The man thought for a moment, then said
"Don't worry, son - God will save me."
The boy shook his head and ran off to the next house.
Sure enough, the waters came pouring down the street and
it wasn't too long before it had risen to a dangerous height.
But out of nowhere, a guy rolls right up to the house
in his little fishing boat and yells through the windows;
"HEY!!!, Get out of there now –
the dam's gonna break any minute !"
And... the man yelled back
 "Thanks, but God will save me !"
Off went the boat to pick up less stubborn hold outs.
Within the hour, sure enough - the dam broke free and by this
time the man was on his rooftop, clutching the chimney.
Over the roar of the waters came a louder sound; a helicopter !
The co-pilot yelled through a bullhorn as he began lowering
a sling; "Grab the rope - we've got to get you out of here !"
To which the man yelled back; "Don't worry ! God willllll..."
and then he was swept off the roof by a wave, and drowned.
Well, when this man made it to the pearly gates of Heaven
- he was ticked !He made his way to the Throne and said;

"God ! I trusted you to save me -
all my life I've trusted you, yet lost
everything AND my life. Why, God ?!?!"

And God said; "I sent you a messenger, I sent you a boat
and even a helicopter. WHAT MORE DID YOU WANT ?!?!? "

All right, my friends both met and unmet; when the storms of Life
rise to meet you - are you blindly looking only for YOUR solution?
Do you continually overlook that which does not
resemble what you were hoping would rescue you?

There are few things more frustrating to me than to see people -
good people, fumble their way through their challenges "their" way -
because that's what's familiar - it's what they know.

News flash:
Familiar and common actions bring familiar and common results,
which typically bring you more of the same that you already have!

The horse and buggy may have been the way to travel before 1910,
but if you want to get anywhere these days - you'd better drive a car.

"I don't know how to drive a car" - Learn

"I have so much invested in horses" - Continually pouring
resources into outdated vehicles is wasting - not investing.

"But I like horses" - Enjoy misery and justifying your failures.

Sounds a bit harsh, doesn't it ?

But really - people will fight tooth & nail against that which
does not fit into their "mold" of an answer or solution.

News flash 2: If they had the solutions –
they wouldn't be having the challenges.
It all boils down to fear: Specifically,
fear of the unknown / Fear of change.

So if the solution to a challenge is unfamiliar, it is typically feared.
And fear is an intangible emotion that has no direct control
over what we can or cannot do. That is worth repeating.

Fear is an intangible emotion that has no
direct control over what we can or cannot do.

I'm going to end with that. We live in a changing world. Be open to it,
accept it, and build on it. Because I'm willing to bet
you've had at least one messenger in your Life.

Are you waiting for a helicopter?
A hydroplane?? Maybe a hovercraft ???

WHAT ARE YOU WAITING FOR ?!?!?

What Children Can Teach US

A while back now, my son & I were at IHOP, which not all that
long ago I learned stood for 'International House of Pancakes'.
DON'T LAUGH ! I don't get out much :)P
We had our fingers crossed that a certain young lad about the
same age as my son would be there as he was the last week.
Why? Well, the week before when we were there this
youngster and his mother came in and he's got a DS
(known in the Young World as a Nintendo DS -
a hand held gaming device that has linking capabilities).
Well, my small fry saw that & was psyched !
He asked me if I could get his DS out of the Jeep,
and long story short these two were soon
playing games & having THE most fun :)
We kept them up far later than good parents should ;)~

So, as you can see, it was with eager anticipation we
were there again :) We ordered food. No sign of them.
The food came & went, and no show. Blah.
My son was getting tired & I gave us 10 more minutes to
head home. Then suddenly: POOF!!! The lil rascal appeared
out of nowhere and slid into the seat next to us!
YAYs and mental high fives all around :)P
After the eating and much playing, there came a point when
I could tell the excitement & pancake syrup were wearing off
and fatigue & low blood sugar were kicking in.
 (My son gets cranky & grumpy when tired or hungry.)
His frustration with trying to play new games was
beginning to show and I knew it wouldn't be long
before the show would need to come to an end.

Now here is why I'm writing this.

My son's new found friend was an inspiration

for the human race – a role model for humanity.

When my son was being withdrawn & unhappy, this kid clued in.

He tried to find other games that he might want to play.

He asked what was wrong - and not in that agitated way

that so many adults ask: "What's wrong with you?!?!??!"

He was genuinely concerned and wanted to know so

that he could somehow help out of compassion.

He offered to show him how to play -

he totally went all out to make my son happy again.

It was both moving & inspiring to see - and it was

everything I could do to not stand up and shout

"Do you know how amazing and incredible you are being ?!?!?!"

I had to call an end to the night because I know when

my son has gone over the edge with no hope of return.

Yet even though the night ended on a not so happy note,

I was thrilled to have seen such a remarkable display

of caring, concern & compassion from a child.

Had any of you been there, you'd have been proud !

And once again, though we as parents

are to be the teaching and training voices

and examples to our children, sometimes

the most valuable lessons ~ are learned from them…

At The End Of Your Rope

When situations become unbearable
and circumstances are overwhelming -
what or who is the knot in your rope
that keeps you from falling off the edge?

There are no right or wrong answers here -
but there had better be an answer, so look deep.
Is it a faith or belief system you have (religious or not)?
Do you have an unshakeable self esteem or self love?
Are there people in your Life who are so important to you
that you would not only give your life for them, but also live it?
What is it for you that keeps you from slipping;
what or who picks you up when you fall?

For myself, there have been many knots added through the years;
knots made by faith & belief, others out of passion & purpose.
Over the years still more knots tied by those who have given me
strength when I was weak, wisdom where I was a fool,
and compassion when I was cold and alone.
These are knots tied out of and with Love -
the kind that can never fray or unravel;
knots made to last a Lifetime...

Now, I'd like to ask you to do something for me,
and someone you don't know. Will you share?
Some time ago I ordered cards made
that had two hands holding a globe.
On them is imprinted:
" UnleashYourselves.com "
and underneath it reads:

"Because everyone has a story to share
that could make a difference… Will you share ? "

I believe that, with all my heart -
and even if you don't think the things you'd have to say
would help someone; trust me when I tell you THEY WILL !!!
There is someone who needs to hear it -
and what you share may be the knot
that will be tied at the end of their rope.

Please take a moment to give to someone
who neither I nor anyone else may reach.
It matters… It will make a difference…

What is your knot ?

What Mom Really Said

When my Mom downloaded "Living for a Lifetime"
she printed the entire book out. She is a very avid reader, and I
can't recall an evening where she did not have a book in her hand.
When she got to the story "If You Can't Say Something Nice",
she let me know that I hadn't quite got it right what she'd said.
I'd always had it that what she was saying was;
"If you can't say something nice, Don't say anything at all."
In actuality, it was: "If you can't say something nice
about someone, Don't say anything at all."
How I wish EVERY person's would follow this rule !

Because I can't stand GOSSIP !!!

I think we all know a few people who just go on and on
about what this person did that was awful, or what
that person did that was simply scandalous.
They seem to feed on and regurgitate the garbage
that they either find or make up about other people.
News flash:
IF they are saying that to you about other people,
chances are GREAT that they are saying the same
kind of things about YOU to those or other people !
I heard something years ago that is just priceless:

> "Don't tear anything down
> unless you're prepared to build
> something better in its place"

Above all, this should apply to people.

Wouldn't it be great the next time someone tries to
unload something negative about someone else -
to stop them and say something nice about them instead?
Because after you do that 2-3 times in a conversation,
the person is going to stop bashing that other person.
AND what if the basher actually begins to believe
that maybe there is something better to be said
about that person than simply spreading junk?

Here's what I know to be true.
If you believe in someone, or believe something about them
there is a strong chance that they will come to believe as well.
In this, they will begin to think and act in a manner that is
congruent and conductive to BEING that which they BELIEVE.

Since this applies to both the Good and the Bad -
let's do our best to discover and bring out the best
in others in order to create a better world for everyone.

And by the way - IF you cannot find something nice to say
about someone, this says far more about you than them.

See what is there to find -
not what you are looking for...

What Song Takes You Back?

I'm sitting here listening to the song "Tim McGraw" by Taylor Swift.
As it does every time I hear it, I think of a song that takes me back
to a place that I'll never forget. For me, it's "Boys of Summer"
by Don Henley. It was popular around the time I was a sophomore
in high school. I had the opportunity to spend Christmas break
in Sarasota, FL. with my best friend & his family. We stayed at
at his aunt & uncle's. Now, I don't remember them at all -
but I do remember their daughter ;) Donna.
You know, like the song by Richie Valens: "I had a girl,
Donna was her name. Since she left me, I've never been the same".

Meanwhile, back in Florida. It must have been the morning after
we arrived (having driven all the way from Indiana) and we were
just getting ready for the day. All of a sudden, she walked in.
My best friend introduced her to me as his cousin.
She was a junior :]~ (this means a year older!)

Through the day, darting eyes and shy glances soon turned into
long gazes and blushes. It's crazy how Life hands you some of
your best memories. One night we were sitting on a park bench at
the beach, just talking and enjoying the chance to finally be alone.
The moonlight made the white sand look like snow, the air was
sharp with the salt of the sea, and the breeze was slightly chilly
against the otherwise warm night. And somewhere during
star gazing and a lull in conversation, our eyes locked.
I felt my heart pound fiercely as neither she or I looked away.
The earth stopped spinning; time stood still. As if in slow motion,
our lips found each other. Clumsily at first, then more and
more instinctively as our ignited passion took over.
Can I even put into words the feeling ?

How does one describe the kind of kissing that shuts out the world
and arouses every sense of one's heart, body, soul and passion ?
Even now - just thinking of it has my pulse racing and
my mind intoxicated. After all - this was my first real kiss !
It was only her curfew that kept us from spending an eternity
together that night. We held hands over the center console
of her blue AMC Eagle wagon on the drive back.

The rest of my vacation was spent doing things with everyone
that should have been "fun", but my mind & heart was completely
consumed by thoughts of her. Every opportunity we could be
around each other, we were. Puppy love...
and I was deep under its spell.

I don't really remember much about leaving.
More than likely it will forever be a mental block for me.
You know how very painful experiences can be.
We wrote each other A LOT, even talked on the phone a few times.
She sent me a picture of herself, and I kept it with me. Always.
She was even going to come up and visit me on spring break !
Puppy love...?

As the weeks turned into months, the distance of miles
began to slowly create distance in our hearts.
Spring Break came and went without her,
and somewhere along the way there was
a final tear stained letter that shared
what we had both known by then
was to be our future.

It's been over three hours that I've sat here writing this - still
listening to Taylor Swift sing me her own bittersweet memories.
You've just let me tell you a part of my Life I've never shared.
The most I think I've ever told anyone is that she was
my first real kiss. Of course, that's all I was going to say
to begin with. My intent was to share how a song can
remind us of good times, happiness, etc...
Tonight I had the opportunity to truly relive
one of the happiest times of my Life; I was there...
My eyes saw hers - and again we did not look away.
I felt her chin in my hand, tasted her sweet lips...
In our embrace we held an eternity of bliss - and it was real.

So if you ever hear me crank the stereo when "Boys of Summer"
is playing and get that far away look in my eyes -
just smile and know that I am in a very happy place...

What song takes you back ?
Let it play in your Life... a lot :)

What Would You Ask For?

The other night I found myself in a restaurant
that I had never been before, and was inspired
by an example of living unreasonably.
There was a man & woman sitting at the booth
diagonally across from me, and I couldn't help
but be both amazed and inspired when she ordered.
She was a redhead. Oh, maybe not originally –
we're talking about the kind of red inspired by
"Hey – I like fire trucks and WOW – I want THAT color red !!!"
She ordered waffles, and she wanted her waffles crisp.
Crisp. CRISP.
The waitress said there was a timer on the cooker,
so she wasn't sure if they could cook them
long enough for them to "crisp".
The woman told the waitress to have them
bypass the timer or reset the time and start over –
whatever it took. Then she let her know that
if they were NOT crisp, then she would
be sending them back.
Now, none of this was said in a mean
or demanding way, yet it was stated firmly.
Almost matter-of-factly, as if she did not expect
there to be a problem, and understood
it may seem like an uncommon request.

When the waffles finally arrived, they were
met with sincere and hearty approval.
Toward the end, while her male companion
was in the bathroom, she asked the waitress
for the bill, then asked if she would just run
the credit card and bring back the receipts.
(The bills are supposed to be paid at the register)
When her friend got back to the table
and asked where the bill was, she stated
it was taken care of and not to worry about it.

He started to protest, but one more
"Don't worry about it – it's done." and
his protests trailed off into "Thank you."

The timing of this was just awesome -
and it just reminded me again that
if we never ask, we'll never get:
and if we shoot for the stars
we might just get the moon…

What Would You Write?

Apparently just the right way to start this isn't in the cards tonight,
so I'm just going to keep writing here & see where we go.

For a while now I've had the idea bouncing around in my head
that if I were to be locked in a room with a laptop & a hundred
or so country songs to lay - I'd walk out with a book.
I say that, because as much as many people make fun of
country music (myself included up until a few years ago) -
the lyrics & story of so many are simply incredible.
Oh, by the way if you don't like country I hope
you're not going to let that check you out now.
Hang in there - don't wimp out ! :P

Tonight I've been playing a song called "If You're Reading This"
by Tim McGraw for about the past 45 minutes. I heard it for the
first time a few weeks ago. It's only been tonight that I read
completely through the lyrics. You see, when I listen to it,
I hear what it invokes within me more than I really get the
words of the song. In this case, a man (soldier) has written
a farewell letter of sorts to his wife in the event of his death.
Here it is for you to read:

"You're reading this, my mama's sittin there
Look's like I only got a one way ticket over here
I sure wish I could give you one more kiss
War was just a game we played when we were kids
Well I'm layin down my gun and hanging up my boots
I'm up here with God and we're both watching over you

245

So lay me down

In that open field out on the edge of town

And know my soul

Is where my mama always prayed that it would go

And if you're reading this... I'm already home

If you're reading this halfway around the world

I won't be there to see the birth of our little girl

I hope she looks like you - I hope she fights like me

And stands up for the innocent and the weak

I'm layin down my gun and hanging up my boots

Tell dad I don't regret that I followed in his shoes

So lay me down

In that open field out on the edge of town

And know my soul

Is where my mama always prayed that it would go

And if you're reading this... I'm already home

If you're reading this, there's gonna come a day

When you'll move on and find someone else, and that's ok

Just remember this I'm in a better place

Where soldiers live in peace and angels sing Amazing Grace

So lay me down

In that open field out on the edge of town

And know my soul

Is where my mama always prayed that it would go

And if you're reading this.. If you're reading this..

I'm already home"

(End)

I have thoughts, but for now I think
 I'll just ask you what you would write.

Have you ever thought about it ?
What letter would you write to those
you would leave behind in this Life ?
I don't know exactly what I would write, so I'm in the same boat you
are. Things that come to mind; ... are going to stay there for now.
Because as I'm thinking with you right now, my list sounds more
like a laundry list of regrets - and that's not the message I want to
leave behind. APPARENTLY my time is not yet near,
which is good news :) Ah, but I'm not letting YOU
off the hook (like I do myself so many times)
I still want to know what your 'letter left behind' will say.
And not the one you think you'll write in 10 years -
or that you'd like to write "someday".
I'll give you three days. And send me your letters :)
You'll know how to find me... When you're ready.

What You Look For
Will Determine
What You See

It's 1:15am on what was a Wednesday night
until Thursday morning took over.
I'm sitting in Shari's restaurant watching the door.
Very few people coming & going.
Sane people are sleeping on a work / school night.

A girl walks in dressed in black, might be 16.
Dark circles under her reddened eyes, pale skin.
Probably goth, maybe just a punk.
No doubt hanging with the wrong crowd,
doing drugs & who knows what else.
Oh yeah, school night.
More than likely a high school dropout.
Why these kids want to live like this
& waste their lives is just beyond me.

And so I pass judgment,
my own fears & opinions painting the canvas
with so many shades of bias, prejudice, and cynicism.
If Beauty is in the eye of the beholder;
does not the opposite hold true ?
This girl - she has a name, and if I had taken the time
to smile instead of scorn in smug reproach
I might have learned it.

Rather than dismiss her as a worthless outcast,
I could have found out that she spent the night
in turmoil anguishing over the recent death of her mother.
The funeral only hours ago a sad ceremony of her loss...
Ever been to the funeral of your mother or father,
who was also your best friend ? It has that effect.
Bloodshot eyes a testimony of her presence
at the hospital day & night...

Now I see a beautiful young Lady - full of love and Life
- sad and grieving for the precious woman who gave her life.

I drain the last of my coffee.
My eyes are getting tired. It's 2:15am
But I can't stop thinking about her.

I've always felt that in some way we learn from everyone we meet.
Now I am reminded that there are also lessons to be learned
from anyone - stranger to soulmate; friend and foe.
Tears and tragedies can become Treasures and triumphs;
the beauty is there for all to behold.

What you look for will determine what you see...

When We Give,
So Much More
We Receive

One night I was at my brother's and he pulled 2 huge
garbage bags full of aluminum cans out of the dumpster
to put them into the recycling bins where they belonged.
Wait a minute. We live 10 minutes from Oregon, where
those cans would add up to some decent pocket change !
Ah, a new adventure for my son and I.
He loves putting the cans into those machines :)
So we loaded them in the back of the Jeep and made for the border.

When we finally located a store that would accept them,
the line was long. We waited for about 10 minutes.
As I was watching, one young man stood out from the rest.
A still small voice inside said "You don't need these; pass them on".
I looked at my son and told him "Change of plans - we're going to
give these to someone who needs them more than we do."
He liked that idea better :)

I got out of the Jeep to get the cans out of the back, and I hesitated.
Was I being judgmental in assuming that guy was there
only for the money and not simply because recycling cans
was the "right" and environmentally responsible thing to do?
Was this his way of giving back to the Earth
and reducing his "footprint" upon the planet?
Would he be insulted that I thought he "needed" my charity?
I kid you not, I got back in the Jeep.

I sat there for another 5 minutes, thinking about many of the things
that had been said the previous day about a total stranger buying
a gift card for a very young couple with 5 very young children
at the restaurant I was in a few weeks ago.
The man who received the gift card (anonymously) was upset
and angry about it, and showed no appreciation, only scorn.
I'd shared this with others to see what they thought, and where
I saw an act of kindness, many others saw judging, belittlement,
and everything but an amazing gesture of generosity for Man.

The final straw for me was thinking about what kind
Of role model I was being to and for my son.
Was I going to back down because I was
afraid of what someone else might think?
Was I going to not do what I believed was the right thing
to do because other's opinions and past experiences
did not agree with mine? Was I going to hesitate in
the face of an opportunity to do the right thing?
I think I've done enough of that over my Lifetime.
So I got back out of the Jeep, grabbed the cans
out of the back and put them in a grocery cart .
I wheeled it up on the curb near him, and said;
"Hey - I've got 2 huge bags of cans right here.
Do you want them?" His eyes lit up, and he said
without any hesitation "I'll take 'em off your hands!"
I said "They're all yours" and he grabbed them and
added them to his cart, thanking me profusely
and wishing us a good night.

What he gave me was worth far more
than the value of those cans.
He reminded me to again appreciate what I have -
no matter how little or how much.
To know that however "bad" we think we have it,
there are countless numbers of people who
would give their right arm to be in our shoes.
Lastly, to take action toward doing what we can for others -
even if it might not seem like much, because I'd rather fault
on the side of helping my fellow man than sitting by in apathy...

Because what's more important;
hurting someone's feelings or pride -
or helping change a Life for the better ?

I hope you and I always choose to do the right thing,
no matter what others may think, no matter how often
your deeds may go seemingly unappreciated or rejected.
Trust me - those moments are few and far between.
And even if the intended recipient doesn't "get" the Gift -
you never know who may be watching and who may have
needed to see that there is still love and kindness in action.

Who You Are To Me

I was driving around today looking for a fun place
to take my son to play. At one point, I looked back at
him and remembered a line from the movie "The Seventh Sign"
that said; "Would you die for Him ?"
So my thought was out of context, for in the movie the
reference was about Christ. And yet it made me think;
Yes, I would not hesitate to die for my son -
there are those things in Life worth dying for.

Still greater, though - What am I willing to live for ?

What am I willing to give; to devote my Life to ?
Is that a question we can honestly say
we've asked - and answered ?

So what is it ?
What is it you feel so passionately about,
that you would devote the rest of your days to ?
What is worthy of devoting the rest of your Life to ?
Are you doing it?
I suspect most people are not. Yes, yes - 1 finger points at you,
and 3 are pointing back at me :) Many of us are doing
things we like to do, but is it really pulling us - calling to us?
Take a brief plunge with me and clear the slate.
Take your job, career, business, occupation
and throw it out the window - even if you like it.
Take $34,000,000 and put half into a savings
account and half into your checking account.
Take your calendar and toss it into the trash.
Now what are you going to do - What is worth your Life?

How would you spend your time?

What would you do with those precious minutes

that go by - never to be captured again?

I want to live my life every day knowing

that because I'm alive - the lives of others are happier.

If I'm in the grocery store, I want to see a smile reflected

back from someone who couldn't seem to find one on their own.

When I'm walking down the sidewalk, I want to see a gleam

in the eye of the passerby because I said Hello; and they

know that I was glad they were there for me to greet.

A kind word, a sympathetic nod;

a smile, a laugh, a handshake, a hug...

A bridge between souls to make a difference.

I may never know what you are going through.

(Yes, you who are reading this.)

Just like I may never know what that stranger walking down

the store aisle looking sad is thinking, contemplating, deciding.

But what if...

What if the road they're traveling

is headed toward destruction.

And what if it only took a moment

of someone caring about it - about them

to head them back to a life worth living ?

I suspect you and I have saved a few lives

and never even known it. At the very least,

we've made a life better by being in it.

I can't believe that if you've spent the time to read this
- ESPECIALLY if you've read everything else in here
that you aren't already one who spreads sunshine
in your own piece of the world around you.
And you know, I had a point in mind
when I started this, but now as I step back
and read it, I think I just want to say thanks.
Thank YOU for living a Life that's
making a difference in others.
It may not be your passion or drive in Life,
but it's important enough for you to take action.

Because of that, I am moved by who you are...

Who You Think You Don't Need To Tell

One evening I received a card from my brother.
Very few words, but seldom have I been as touched.
It said;

" Rob -

      Every single day I appreciate you.

        Thank You

      Love,

        Chris "

Chris is my twin brother. And sure, we both know
there isn't anything we wouldn't do for the other, etc...
but it's something that really isn't said.
And yet, it's been 6 hours
and each time I read it I get teary eyed.
I guess sometimes we need to hear that,
and maybe I've needed to hear it more than I knew.

How many people go days, weeks, years without
someone telling them how they are appreciated,
how much they mean to them; how much they are loved.
We take so much for granted.
We tell ourselves "They know I care"
instead of saying it to the other person.

I recall it was but a few years ago that I actually told
my parents that I loved them. I think it was 2003.
I remember calling them with the intent to say it.
And I chickened out.
So I called back and told my Dad that
I only pretended to call earlier for whatever reason.
And I got to tell him that the real reason I had called
was to tell him that I loved him. Since then, all of our calls
end with both my parents and myself saying "Love you".
And I'm always aware how much I mean it when I do.
There's never been a question about it - but it's rarely been said.
Always assumed; taken for granted - a given.

So why say it ? Why tell someone you're thinking of them?
Why call an old friend and tell them you were just thinking
about them and that you're glad they're in your Life?
Because words heal, and often, time has a way of numbing wounds.
They are the evidence - the expression of what is inside.
How do you feel when someone says
something nice to you - and means it?
How does it make you feel when someone says:
"I don't think I tell you enough
how much you mean to me".
Has anyone ever said that?

For myself, I become very aware that it really is
good to be alive; and I think the world of the
person who shared their message with me.
People you know suffer quietly every day, starving
for acknowledgment, for appreciation, for love.

The impact you can have with a few words
can echo for generations. You can be the
catalyst and the cause in changing the world.
As farfetched as this may seem at first,
a ripple in the heart of humanity
can change the face of the earth.
And to those around you,
you are already making an impact
- by what you say, and don't say.

All I ask of you is not to forget anyone...
and begin with those closest to you
who you think don't need to be told.

Why ?

Because of you.

Tonight has found me once again editing my website and
so I've decided to answer the unasked question of "Why?"
Now, the first three words of this paragraph should be sufficient,
but you will come to know soon enough that I have to explain
my answers & explanations with more answers & explanations.
:P
And yet... it really is because of you.

Before I ever began posting anything online,
the "audience" of my Life was minute to say the least.
(Those who know me can tell you how anti-social I am)
Then through various online mediums, you and others found me,
and vice versa. Slowly I began sharing some of my thoughts,
all the time wondering what you would think of me.
And you let me know !!!
...and I've never been more humbled.

What I've come to realize is that what I have shared
has made a positive impact in many people's lives,
and that what I say does matter to people.

Most of you will never know how big that is for me.

So the creation of UnleashYourselves.com was born
out of a desire to both share AND have others share
thoughts, experiences, ideas, and inspirations that
could be passed onto the World around us.

I know so many of you have some incredible things to
share with others - You've shared many of them with me !
So I've got to tell you
the same thing I realized for myself;

What you say matters.

In order to change the World around us,
we must begin by changing the world within.

Unleash yourselves...

~Robert H. Steffen
September 14, 2008

Why Throw Away Treasure?

Recently I've had a few discussion about... ex'es
(or is it "exes", "ex's", or "exi" as in more than one "ex" ???)

So here's my theory. People are people, and we all have
things about us that rub some people the right way,
and things that rub them & others the wrong way.
Of the billions of people in this world, we have the
opportunity to actually meet with but a fraction of them.
Within that group we will find some that we are attracted to
or interested in on some level. I am not even talking about
boy/girl | man/woman attraction; but simply people having
traits, attributes & characteristics that we like. I've always had
the notion of that being sort of the doorway to friendship.
So, we get to know these people - each of us sharing with the
other and becoming more and more familiar with each other.
In this process, we either grow closer and more connected,
or those things about them (or us) that are disliked outweigh
the positive attributes that caught our attention in the first place
and we drift away. Either way, we've had the chance to become
part of another's world, and for them to have shared in ours.
Either way a blessing ! After all, isn't one the basest cravings
of human nature the desire for attention & affection ?

Now we get to the sticky part.
Where Man and Woman are concerned,
this friendship process can and very often
leads to a relationship that includes intimacy
and romance. FANTASTIC ! Do you realize
how precious few of these experiences
we will have in our lifetime ?!?

For myself, I have never felt as alive, appreciated
or loved as when in a romantic relationship.

And still, because a friendship becomes romantic
and intimate does not mean that there won't be
those things that we dislike about the other.
They just have a tendency to be overshadowed
or hidden by the feelings that we enjoy far more
that involve passion, romance, and intimacy.
Yet those little things that bother us we come to realize
are but the tips of icebergs, and eventually we see that
the level of long term compatibility cannot continue.

STOP !
This is the part that I have a hard time with.
Most of the time people will take this incredible person,
cast them aside and want nothing further to do with them.
Hello?!? What about all of the things about them
that drew us to them in the first place? Unless
they were just a fake & lying schmuck, those
things are still there - a part of that person !
So, let me get this straight.
Here we meet someone who we like
and they have enough positive things
about them for us to continue giving and
sharing ourselves to the highest levels,
            and we just toss them away ?!??

They are still a PERSON !
And simply because a few aspects
of the relationship didn't "work out" –
why throw away the whole treasure ?

If I dug up a treasure chest on the beach,
and it was filled with gold, rubies, emeralds
and five silver bars - am I going to bury it
just because I don't care for silver bars?
 Of course not !
Those silver bars do not make
the treasure any less priceless;
and for another may well be
of greater value than the gold...

If someone could treat me so casually
and not appreciate the value of who I am
as a person - regardless of the "status"
of the relationship, then I fear I have made
a grave error in choosing them as someone
I could be a friend with in the first place.
No... I can't even say that;
for just because they choose
to throw away treasure does not mean
that I have to lose the treasure of who they are.
All in all it just saddens me that so many lives
are allowed to casually slip from our Life when
there is still so much that is good we can share...

So this may sound an odd thing to say,
but if I ever share my Life with you in any way
it means that you are a treasure to me -
no matter what "level" or "status".

Will You Give Your Life
or Live Your Life?

So... have you ever had that feeling
that something really big is going to happen
and you don't know what it is —
only that it's important?
That's where I'm at right now.
Somewhere between now and the final words
there is something so important and big
that I don't even know where to begin -
or how to describe how badly
I need to share it with you.

Now, some time ago I had mentioned...
No. You know what ?
Let's just begin as if you
don't know anything about me.

I'm the father of a now 7 year old boy,
who has truly given me a bigger heart and
a deeper capacity to love than I ever had
before he came along. And, like most
any parent, I'd give my Life for him.
For those I love and care for, I would
sacrifice my life if it meant saving theirs.

If you've been in the military, or consider
yourself patriotic, I'd be willing to bet
you'd give your Life for your Country.

For whatever cause we believe deeply enough in,
there can be no greater expression of it
than to sacrifice one's Life for it.
EXCEPT...
Living your Life for it,
instead of giving your Life for it.

Last night I watched a movie called "7 Pounds".
In essence, a man's carelessness caused the death of
7 others in an auto accident. He then dedicated himself
to the cause of creating new lives for 7 other people,
the final price of which was his very Life.
And though I admire his ultimate sacrifice,
I believe there is a greater gift we can give.

What if...
What if we gave our Lives instead of our Life ?

Couldn't we do so much more by giving
of our time, talents, abilities, and resources
over the course of our lifetime ?
And even better - a LONG lifetime at that !

I say yes. And... it just dawned on me:
you may not think you're "that" person.

OK. I've got keep my cool about this
because I do not know you.
Here's what I've discovered about most people.
They have a trailer park mentality.

Why do I call this a trailer park mentality ?

Many years ago I watched a movie called
"The Last Starfighter". One of the greatest
messages in history is in that movie !
Cliff's Notes version.
An alien recruiter (Centauri) comes to Earth
looking for kid (Alex, who lives in trailer park)
who broke the record on an arcade game
that was actually a fight simulator. After a
somewhat cryptic "motivational" message
from Centauri to Alex – Alex responds with;

"I'm not any of those guys,
I'm a kid from a trailer park."

and Centauri says:

" **If that's what you think,**
then that's all you'll ever be ! "

Now, it is with the greatest amount of self control
that I do not scream at you right now and tell you
that I don't care if you're a kid from a trailer park
or the Vice President of the United States.
I don't care if you're a high school dropout
washing dishes at night to feed your 3 kids -
or if you've won the Nobel Peace prize... twice.
You DO have what it takes to alter
the course of not only your Life but
especially the lives of others as a result.

So why wouldn't you ?
Seriously - knowing that you can,
why wouldn't you ??

Again, staying calm here - but do me this
favor and wrap your head around this:

IF YOU KNEW
YOU COULD CHANGE THE WORLD,
WHY WOULDN'T YOU ?

I've got to say that if you're reading this and
you've read this far down the page -
the ONLY reason a person like you wouldn't
is because you probably think
 you're just a kid from a trailer park.
You don't think you're "all that".

Great.
Then at least we can see eye to eye.
Because there's one more thing I know
about you if you're reading this right now.

You've got far more potential to make an impact
on the world around you than I ever will.

Don't even try to tell me different -
just accept it, and stop making excuses.
(And if you dwell on this point, you are missing it)

Listen to me very very closely.

YOU have the ability to make a positive and
meaningful impact in the lives of those around you.
That's not an opinion.
It's not something I'm just saying to make you
or anyone else feel good or warm & fuzzy.
Quite frankly the fact that it's true
is a real source of frustration to me
and keeps me up most nights.

You're not just a kid from a trailer park.

You're not just a guy working behind a counter.
You're not just a gal answering phones.
You're not just ...
What you are is a miracle
of virtually untapped potential
waiting to be discovered and unleashed.

Now what will you do
to move the World around you
now that you and I know you can ?

And dare I ask
would you give your life to loving,
living, and giving the gift that is your Life ??

Would You Change A Thing?

There is something that has made me question
anything and everything that has happened in my Life
and where and what those things have brought me.

It goes far deeper than what I'm going to touch on,
but I don't think you have the many hours
to read what I'd really like to say here,
so let's just start with a simple question:

Can you think of a happy time in your life ?

Or let's say this;
think of an event that made you incredibly happy.

Now,
What were you doing the day before ?

So let's take it back further...

What about the events of the week prior to ?
How about that month ??
Year ???

Now what if the events leading up
to that moment were changed...

It is most probable that a shift in
that "chain" would detour you from
the happiness you either now experience
or had experienced in the past.

Consider that you may be somewhere
on that timeline, and when you look back
you will understand and appreciate that
everything that happened was merely a
piece of the puzzle - a link in the chain that
brought you to the happiness in your Life.

Some of you...
are going through tough times right now.
I wish - I really do
that you were past them;
that today was a day where
you could look back and be grateful
that you made it through those dark days.

You just have to believe that you will get past them -
that they are part of a tapestry that when finished
will be a Creation of beauty beyond your imagination.

Would You Have Stopped?

It's dark out and I'm driving with my son
across the 205 bridge from Portland to Vancouver.
Actually, I'm doing all the driving – his legs are too short
to reach the pedals and he doesn't have a license yet.
All of a sudden the car stalls and the engine stops.
I'm in a 1966 Datsun Roadster, which used to be my Dad's.
Coasting to the side of the road I'm hoping like heck people
see me (small car – very small) while at the same time
wishing I had a few tools in the car and a flashlight.
And then… a car pulls up behind me.

I smiled that someone was stopping, but doubted they would
be much help. After all, not only is this car rare, but it's had
modifications done to it that many would just shake their head at.
By this time I was fairly certain the fuel pump wasn't working,
because when the key is on and the kill switch enabled there
should be a slightly annoying clicking of the pump.
There was none. Ugh. Did I mention it was dark out and
getting late? AND I am nowhere near any auto parts store,
nor would they be open if I was!

So, while I'm trying to slide under the car that sits about as low
to the ground as a skateboard, this fellow produces a flashlight
to help me see. I happened to have a test light in the trunk,
and was able to discover that the fuel pump was not getting
any power. In my mind this was a relief because I had wired
it in - so it couldn't be TOO complicated to find, right?
Did I mention how low this thing sits to the ground yet?
Argh… Anyway, as I'm poking around testing for power
in the wires, here is what I find out about my Rescuer.

Not only do we share a common flashlight, guess what kind of car he has at home. Yep. A Datsun Roadster. Not one, BUT TWO !!! Apparently one of them is pretty darned nice - as in show car nice, so I felt a bit apologetic for the not so pristine condition of mine. What can I say – I was 10 years old when my Dad hauled it home after paying a mere $65 for it! It's been around the block and halfway across the country. AND, get this – this guy, who I figured at first wouldn't be able to help me, is the head moderator of a Roadster website!! HOW COOL IS THAT ?!?!? I mean, of all people to have seen me and stopped ! ! !

Well, after much crawling around on the ground and trying to squeeze under the car enough to find and follow wires from the back of the car to the front of the car – the culprit turned out to be… a fuse. Yes. A fuse. 1 of 4 easy to see and access fuses under the hood of the car which required no crawling on the ground to open or replace. NOTE TO ALL PEOPLE: CHECK YOUR FUSES FIRST. Those who know me will be giving me endless grief about this, because I've been around cars all my life - and I of all people should have known to look there first and foremost. Apparently I went in looking for the worse case and overlooked the most probable and simplest cause. (How many times do you do that in Life???)

So, I put a new fuse in. Actually, it wasn't "new' per say, as I suspect it's been in there ever since my Dad owned it. Anyway, long story short – the car started right up. I was relieved, though felt rather foolish. After a bit of banter we parted ways - but not before profuse thanks were given, to which he shared that I pay it forward.

Ahhhh… Music to my ears.

Another side to this person I liked :)

I finally tracked him down a few days later from

the website he moderates and I emailed him.

He shared with me this story -

which I'd like you to pay attention to:

" Years ago, I commuted 30 miles each way over Iowa's highways.
US Hiway 30 between Marshalltown and Tama/Toledo was a pretty
straight forward road… with few houses or businesses along it's
length except for the small town of Le Grand (which did have TWO
signs for "Welcome" and "Leaving", but you COULD see the
other one while standing at one.) One day, running late for my job
as Assistant Manager at a bookstore in the Marshaltown mall and
having been scolded by my boss for having run late earlier in the
week, I was pushing the speed limit well past it's breaking point
when I spied a car on the side of the road with a woman looking at
her obviously flat tire. Ordinarily I'd stop, but I was more worried
about my job. So with a prayer that she would get help soon,
I was prepared to pass her by, feeling remorse at my own need
to get to work to keep my job. Just as I was about to draw even
with her car, as I was zipping by, two little kid's heads popped up
in the rear window…. DANG!!! Now I REALLY couldn't pass it by.
I pulled over, and backed up. Her tire wasn't just flat… it was worn
and torn so badly that it wasn't going to be able to repaired
(I had thought to use my fix-a-flat can). Worse yet her spare was
also worn down PAST the threads AND you could see the last
of the rubber starting to bulge out from the worn areas.
I pointed out the problem and told her that I would change it, but
that I would have to follow her into Le Grand to the gas station
so she could possibly purchase a better used tire. I changed the
tire, followed her in and bid good bye at the gas station.

As I left I told her that if she had any more problems, to give me a call at my bookstore and that I was the Assistant Manager there. As luck would have it, my boss was also late and she never realized I'd opened the store 20 minutes late.

Skip forward several months… I had worked late, long past the regular closing time of the mall and was headed home on Hiway 30. Needing to hit the rest area, I took the turn-off and proceeded down the dirt /gravel road only to discover that I had missed the actual entrance to the rest area and was now proceeding down past it. I looked for a place to turn around, in the complete pitch black of a moonless night, on a muddy road with a definite crown to it and run-off ditches on both sides…. with little luck.

Finally about 2 miles in, I spied an access entry into a farm field and I thought I could use it to do a 3 point u-turn. No such luck, I ended up sliding on the mud and ended up with the whole passenger side of the car in the drainage ditch mud.

I got out, and realized that in my nice pants and shoes and as slippery as it was… it wasn't going to happen tonight.

I had a choice, I could sleep in the car and deal with it in the morning, or I could walk back to the road and hope that someone at 11pm plus would give me a ride to a phone (I had AAA).

Just as I was locking up the car, and getting ready to start walking away… a car pulled up. A couple were going into town for a late snack. He asked what had happened and told me to wait a couple minutes and he'd be right back. Thanking my guardian angel, I waited and sure enough, he showed up with a dual-axle pick-up truck and a snatch rope. In just a few minutes (he even attached the rope so I wouldn't get messy), my car was out and ready to roll down the road. I thanked him profusely and offered him a discount at my bookstore since I didn't have any money with which to pay him. He just told me to pay it forward.

Skip ahead another couple of months.

Now it's getting close to Christmastime and the mall is BUSY.
A young woman stops at my register and looks at me long and
patiently. "How may I help you?" I ask. "You don't remember me
do you?" she replies. This really wasn't what I was expecting,
and although I had had a few girlfriends, I was still young enough
to be able to remember them all, so I replied, "No, not really,
how do I know you?". To which she asked,
"Did your car get stuck in a ditch and needed to be pulled out?"
Which of course it had, so now thinking it was the wife of the man
who helped me, I asked her which books she'd like to purchase
and that I would buy them with my employee's discount to save
her and repay them for their kindness. She mentioned that she
wasn't there to buy some books, which left me a bit confused
as to what she was expecting from me. She then related how
I'd helped HER with her car's tire and followed her to the
gas station in Le Grand. That rang a bell but I asked,
"How did you know about my being stuck in the ditch?"
She floored me with her reply,
"That was my Brother-In-Law that pulled you out.
I just wanted you to know that we're all paying it forward
just like you asked me to do when you helped me."

So you see, it really does work. - E.S. "

Awesome.
Come on now - IS THAT AWESOME OR WHAT?!?!?

Now, I was going to ask you to stop reading -
but then you wouldn't know why if you did !

What I really want to know is; ——>
                    Would you have stopped ?

275

Because it might surprise, you who know me,

to know that more times than not I haven't stopped

to help people who I see stopped alongside the road.

My typical excuses are:

* What if it's a trap of some sort; I don't want to endanger my son.

* I don't have tools, so I doubt I could be of much help.

* Someone else will be able to help more than I.

* I'm in a hurry and I don't have time.

And there's the ugly truth of it. I'm sure there are a few more,

but these seem to have worked so far. No wonder I feel guilty

whenever I drive on by – because there is a great deal I do know

about cars, so I probably could help. AND even if I can't fix

the problem I could at least do something that would get

them closer to a solution. Apparently I overlook that.

I mean really, would it be so hard to at least see if they were OK?

A few minutes… To at least make sure there isn't a Life at risk.

That's the least we could do –

and wouldn't we appreciate the same?

So… mind if I ask – What do you use as your excuses?

I'm just asking – no judging; I just told you I'm guilty as heck.

I keep thinking of this:

" **I shall pass this way but once;**

any good therefore that I can do,

or any kindness that I can show -

let me not defer nor neglect it,

for I shall not pass this way again. "

I must say, this past week I've cleaned out the Jeep a bit
and put a few tools in the back – just in case :)

So, let's take this off road and into the path of Life -
where we cross people every day who are broken down
and need help in their lives. Do we even notice?
How quick are we to just speed past; how often do we
simply pass on by the stuck and the stranded around us?
See if this sounds familiar:
* I'm in a hurry and I don't have time.
* Someone else will be able to help more than I.
* I don't have the right tools, so I doubt I could be of much help.

Would you like to know one of the most powerful declarations
that, if embraced and practiced, would be the end of every protest
and riot? It would mean the end of any war and "conflict"
of nations – would solve the strife of the homeless, and
none would go to bed hungry nor hopeless again.

It's this:
(And I wish I had a nickel for every
 one of you who has heard this before)
"Do unto others as you would have them do unto you"
If that sounds too "religious" for some of you, use:
"Treat people the way you'd like to be treated".
If you like religions, try these;
Judaism: "Thou shalt Love thy neighbor as thyself."
Buddhism: "Hurt not others with that which pains yourself."
Confucianism: "What you do not want
done to yourself, do not do to others."
Hinduism: "One should always treat others
as they themselves wish to be treated."

Take your pick, or make one up you like better if you are above
and beyond such "religious" beliefs. Any way you slice it,
you would see a world transformed by the practice
(not just the "preaching") of this idealism.

When I was a kid, my parents at times would ask me
"How would you like it if someone did that to you?"
This usually followed the discovery of something I had done that
was less than desirable behavior. Fast forward to today, and I have
caught myself saying the exact same thing to my son at times.

So now that we're all grown up now - let me ask you;
"How would you like it if someone did that to you?"

How would you like it if people just drove on by
when you were stuck on the side of the road ?
How would you like it if you were on hard times
and people just kept walking by and ignoring you?
How would you like it if you were sad and lonely
and no one bothered to ask you what was wrong?
How would you like it if all you heard was ridicule?
How would you like it if you worked hard
and were never given credit or recognition?
How would you like it if you were at the end of your rope,
and no one stopped to ask how you were doing – and mean it?

What if you had to one day face all of the people
that you could have helped; that you could have
made a real and positive impact on, BUT DIDN'T…
What would you say to them?
I'll bet your reasons and excuses would sound pretty weak.

So how about being the amazing people I know you to be
and step up your game of Greatness and get rid of the
selfish excuses we have for not doing the right thing.
How about taking a couple of weeks and be intent on treating
people as we would want to be treated. I'd say start with those
close to you, but don't get too comfortable there. Work your
way to casual acquaintances; then take the leap toward strangers.
There are far more of them, so it shouldn't be too hard to do…
One other thing. Read this:

The Star Thrower (condensed) by Loren Eisele

"There was a man who was walking along a sandy beach
where thousands of starfish had been washed up on the shore.
He noticed a boy picking the starfish one by one and throwing
them back into the ocean. The man observed the boy for a few
minutes and then asked what he was doing. The boy replied that
he was returning the starfish to the sea, otherwise they would die.
The man asked how saving a few, when so many were doomed,
would make any difference whatsoever? The boy picked up
a starfish and threw it back into the ocean and said
"Made a difference to that one…"
Bending down he retrieved another, tossing it into the waters.
"And that one…" as he continued his rescue mission.
The man left the boy and went home, deep in thought of what
the boy had said. He soon returned to the beach and spent the
rest of the day helping the boy throw starfish in to the sea…."

What you do makes a difference.

So do it...

You And I Are Living Together

Ever had that sort of gnawing thought
in the back of your mind that something was
passing you by and you couldn't quite figure out what?
Sort of like standing on a frozen river;
the part you're standing on is made from the
very same thing that flows beneath you;
yet one moves on, while the other stays.

Now at some point I hope that what I'm thinking is actually going
to find its way to you resembling something that makes sense.
So here we go :)

Did you know that you and I are living together ?
Really - we are;
we are both alive at the same time on the same planet.
And... on top of that, so are "they".
You know who "they" is; anyone that isn't us ! :)P
From the president of my country
to the prostitute on Broadway;
both near and far they and we all have this one thing in common:
Living together. The people around me, the people around you;
THESE are the people that we live with.

From time to time I really grasp the depth of that, which makes me then
wonder how I'm treating them. And... for the most part I'd say that I'm
a good neighbor. I recently moved and as I was packing things up my
neighbor told me that he'd miss me - that I was a good neighbor.
And I laughed and said, "yeah, I'm quiet and I'm never around!" to
which he chuckled and said "Yeah - that's what I meant..."

Ah, but the truth of those words
now echo in my restless mind.
I am quiet, and I'm never around.
And that makes me a good neighbor.

That's not the way I want to be remembered.

As I was going through my wallet tonight looking at
various scraps of paper, on one I had written this:

"It's not because I want to leave something behind.
It's because I want to pass it forward..."

Yet as I read this, I see that what is missing is the Now.
You see, the most important part of you and I living together
and the only reason to bring it up is because it's happening now.
And by now you should realize that now is the only
time we have that we can do anything with.
So, remember earlier when I said that at some point
I hope what I'm thinking is actually going to find its way
to you resembling something that makes sense ?
Well, I think what it all boils down to is this:

Look around you.
THESE are the people you live with -
the people who are in your Life NOW.

Do what you can
to make their World a better place,
and you will have created a better Life for yourself.

You And I Need Bigger Problems

Earlier today while I was at work, a woman came in
whose face had been severely disfigured from burns.
Several times I caught myself avoiding as much eye contact
as I normally would allow because it was distracting.
And if I'm distracted... well, you who know me know I have
to keep starting things over and over again if distracted.

When we were through and she was walking away,
I couldn't help but admire that she didn't allow
what many would perceive as a life-stopping tragedy
to stop her from living, laughing, and enjoying Life.
I also thought about how grateful you and I should be.
Yes, I said you and I .

Today is Monday. Now, I've got be careful not to step on any
toes, because I happen to believe that Life's greatest lessons and
examples not only come from US, but from those around us.
So here is what I believe.
Some time ago I went to the funeral of a dear friend's dad.
I wish I had the opportunity to have known him better,
for he has truly left behind a legacy of love and respect.
What I think I can tell you beyond a shadow of a doubt is
that he would gladly and gratefully trade places with that
woman if he could - and he'd give up anything for the chance.

Now, I don't what it is really, but for the past few months
I've felt like screaming at people to take a reality check and
look at what they HAVE - and stop fussing about all of the
little petty things they are allowing to kill their happiness.
(Because it's really starting to cut into MY happiness ! :p)

Some of you have big... BIG challenges -
and I admire you for how you are handling them.
But I've got to say that most people really need bigger problems -
problems worth their time and energy to really dig in and overcome.
I feel fortunate in that the people I choose to surround myself with
typically aren't prone to let something like a flat tire or broken nail
ruin their day. It's just stuff that happens along the way in this Life.
I look at someone like Martin Luther King Jr. or Abraham Lincoln,
and realize that they just chose to tackle bigger problems than
the majority of those around them who merely complained.
And if you really think about it, they chose to help other
people with their problems - and in doing so made
a huge difference in their own and their World.

Many years ago I heard a very wealthy and respected man
say that if you want to overcome your own problems -
find someone who has a bigger problem than you do, help them
solve it, and not only does their problem go away, but pretty
soon yours doesn't seem like such a big problem after all.

You are alive in the greatest country in the world.
What more could you ask for ?
I mean, really - stop and think about that.
Billions of people would give anything to be in your shoes.
I, and everyone reading this, ought to kiss the ground
and thank God every day that we are alive and free
to overcome the challenges that we face.

You Don't Know What You Don't Know
(revisited)

It's one of those nights again.
You know the one
- where the mind is restless, the body fidgety,
and there's something that just needs to get out...
but you don't know what.
The what is unknown at this time,
but I'm hoping by the time we're done here
we'll know what, and maybe even why.

A short while ago I told you about things
we don't see about ourselves, and I
received some interesting feedback.
Though I loved knowing how you took what I said,
as well as what it evoked from within you;
it also gave me the suspicion that what I had
wanted to convey had slipped through the cracks.
The serendipity of it all is that
now we're both the better for it,
and I'm glad our mental paths separated.

Remember when I said that
you don't know what you don't know ?
Well, when I said that the motivation for it
stemmed from those things in Life that
are detrimental to what it is we want.
The things we don't see - that we don't know
that keep us from where we want to go, have, etc.
I will agree that every experience adds
to the great sum of who we are.

284

In that there is the realization that we might be
"less" than ourselves had we chosen
differently in our Walk of life.
With that in mind, I've also been given
the impression that if we somehow alter
our normal way of being and make conscience
decisions that seem to go against "who we are"
that it means we are not being true to ourselves
and that the beauty of who we are
is somehow tainted and distorted.

What I should have added
to my original conversation
might sound something like this:

"If there are areas of our life in which
we are not completely satisfied and happy with,
then it would benefit us to make decisions that
would lead us toward greater fulfillment in those areas.
* IF that is really what you want.
(*there are always those who would rather defend
a position and/or justify past decisions and actions)"

So back to square one, with hopefully a different view;

There are things that we see and know hold us
Back from achieving a more fulfilling Life.
What usually stands in the way of conquering these
things are the things THAT WE DON'T SEE.
It was the ice UNDER the water that sank the Titanic.

285

Realizing that there are things beneath the surface
that affect who we are, what we do, how we act, react...
That in itself may cast enough light to reveal
the shadow of what really holds us back.
Something else to keep in mind,
and I may have mentioned this before;
often other people can see those things
about us that we are blind to.
So humor me if you will,
and read the original piece (below) again.

...and I'd be very curious to hear if anything shifted

-------- original message ---------

While I was walking down the aisle at a store some
time ago, a rather attractive young lady looked at me,
smiled, and looked away. Well, I thought that was
pretty cool - a nice boost to my ego :)
Of course, I was wearing my lucky sweater.

* I've nicknamed it my lucky sweater because it is
my favorite, lightweight & incredibly comfortable.
It is brown in color and those of you who know me or
have met me have probably seen it by now UNLESS
you met me on a hot day and haven't seen me since.
I will more than likely pass this sacred sweater down
to my son when he is 18, who will be gracious in
its acceptance and either hide it away in his closet
or donate it to Goodwill...

Meanwhile, back at the ranch... or in this case store.

A little while later, a couple of girls smiled at me &
sort of giggled after I had passed.
Flirtatious vixens - probably acting all kinds of silly
when a handsome young lad as myself is near.
My, I was starting to feel like quite the stud!
Even some dude gave me the nod - like I was all
kinds of cool. On the way home I was feeling about
6' 4" and contemplating when I would start booking
my GQ photo shoot and what agency to represent me.

Brace yourselves;
everything is about to come crashing down.

I went into the bathroom after I got home,
looked in the mirror and saw the huge stain of
taco sauce down the left side of my mouth... face.

And it wasn't just your average dark red taco sauce.
This stuff was a very light orange-pinkish colour.
Very very tasty and incredibly messy.

What I learned, aside from remembering to
Wipe that delicious taco sauce off my face
(or should I say what I was reminded of) is

There are things about us that we do not see -
that we do not know.

STOP !

Savor that point.

There are things about us
that we do not see -
that we do not know.

Now, give me an example.
I'll wait.

Make it a good one...

I'm patient.
Seriously - I can wait :)

And you know,
even a small example would be OK...

So... I'm not trying to pressure you or anything,

but I would like to, you know - get to the point...

tonight

sometime...

I just need an example any example, OK ?

OOOoooookay then

- I'm just going to finish this up here while
you're thinking. If you are still thinking &
haven't come up with an example,
that is exactly my point.
If you did manage to find an example - think again.
Tell me something about yourself that you do not know
something about yourself that you do not see.

You can't, because you don't know it's there.
(Or as a very wealthy person once said -
"you don't know what you don't know")

BUT JUST BECAUSE YOU CAN'T SEE IT
OR DON'T KNOW ABOUT IT
DOESN'T MEAN IT'S NOT THERE.

It doesn't mean that it's not having an effect
on your Life and on those around you.
Quite the contrary:

all too often it's the things
that we are not aware of
that determine and dictate so much
of what we do and do not do.

With that in mind,

there is a very good chance all your efforts

thus far are done to affect and have an effect

only on that which you are aware of and see.

You and I are all aware of the things

we do know and suspect are causing and

creating both our victories and our failures;

yet when we hit a wall and find ourselves unable

to move forward - there are things of which we

are not aware, things that we are blind to seeing

and knowing, that are continually tripping

us up and making us fall and fail...

Realizing this is the first step

to seeing what you are looking for and finding it...

Your Life Is An Occasion

I often wonder what you were doing
before you start reading this.
Taking a quick break from work perhaps,
or maybe getting caught up on emails
and such just before bed.
Perhaps you're peering over
your morning cup of coffee.

The reason I ask is because I wonder
where your mind is - and what you might be
expecting to find between the words and the lines..

So tonight these words are bouncing around in my head
"Your Life is an occasion; Rise to it."

Those of you smiling may recognize this as a
quote from "Mr. Magorium's Wonder Emporium".
I just watched it tonight (2nd time) at the invite &
encouragement of someone who must've known
it may be just the thing I needed to hear.

You know, we hear that phrase "rise to the occasion"
typically around important & pivotal events -
opportunities that would call us & require us
to act and do more than is expected.

At this time I feel the need
to tell you something very important -
something I hope you will remember
each and every morning you wake up.

YOUR Life is the greatest occasion -

the most important event

you will ever experience.

I don't care how much you know,

your level of education or your occupation.

I don't care who you know or where you live.

I don't care the numbers of your age or your bank account.

YOUR Life is

the greatest occasion -

the most important event

you will ever experience.

Are you rising to the occasion?

Are you living as though your Life

actually mattered in this World ??

And if you do know, are you sharing it ?

You Will Soon Witness A Miracle

"You will soon witness a miracle. "
These are the words that stared up at me from a
fortune cookie one night/morning at 4:15am,
and my first thought was "Yes, me finishing this
before sunrise!", which was soon replaced
by the title of one of my favorite books:
"The Greatest Miracle in the World" by Og Mandino.
If I had my way, you would borrow, buy or steal
a copy & read it. What I will also share is that,
like most things, you should read it via the
shopping cart method. Meaning, if you don't
understand or agree with something you read –
don't just toss it or throw the whole thing out.
Gather what you can use and let your mind feast :)

Now…
I want you to do me a favor
and really really think this through.

If you found out that you were not only a miracle,
but THE greatest miracle in the world;

How would your Life change ?

Would you settle for a mundane & average day,
or would you demand the best and not settle for less ?
Come on now – really get it; Let it sink in:
" YOU are the greatest miracle in the world ".
Picture it… grasp it… let your mind embrace it.

I remember reading that when I was about 23yrs old,
and I never forgot it. The seed of that realization
planted itself deep within those parts of me
that thought I was anything but.
Ah, but I'm still wondering about you.
If I could actually convince you of this,
what spectacular achievements and dreams
would you actually set forth to conquer –
because as the greatest miracle in the World
you certainly deserve to get them… and more.

So while you're considering the
implications and possibilities of you
being the greatest miracle in the world,
grab a paper & pen and start making
a list of what you'd undertake…

When finished, find a mirror
and gaze upon your reflection.
"You will soon witness a miracle. "

Done.

The Homeless

It was a fun night celebrated with friends that brought
me to downtown Portland. That's the Oregon one
(pronounced Or-ree-gahn by the out of towners) -
not the one in Maine on the OTHER coast.
It was on the walk back to the car that I saw it.
The "it" was a bundle of blankets in a doorway.
No. There was more. "It" was more than that.
There was a person wrapped up in those blankets.
Not an "it". A "Who".
A Who was bundled up in blankets in the
doorway of a building that I was walking by.
I was walking by.
We were walking by.
Others were walking by.
Everyone... was walking by...

I haven't stopped thinking about it.
I just can't get rid of the vision of a man
tired of walking, tired of wandering; a man
with nothing left but the clothes on his back.
He is hungry... he is cold... he has no place of his own...

At what point did he realize that he would need to find blankets,
clothing, and rags to cover himself just to stay warm that night ?
What time did he finally give out, choosing that doorway
as home and the concrete as his bed?
And then I wonder at what point was that his new "normal"...

The "American Dream"... epic fail.

The further I walked,
the more of "Them" I saw.

I wondered how many of those silent Souls were
women and children - whose prayers before
sleep were that they live to see the morning.
And I couldn't help wonder if there were those
whose prayers were that they would not.

Can you imagine?
No, really - Can you?
Come daylight, they worry about where to hide
what little they have and where to find food to eat.
We see them doing what they can to survive -
with a mix of pity and compassion, tempered
only by quick and quiet judgment.
Would you judge me if I told you that I've stood in
food lines for a hot meal and then picked through the
free bread bins hoping to find wheat instead of white?
Would you think less of me if I said that I went to
churches to pick up food boxes to feed my family?
Maybe you didn't know.
Things are often not what they seem,
and appearances can be so deceiving.
Besides, your eyes were probably elsewhere...

As I walked that night, I did not need to raise my
eyes far to see the homes not far up the hill whose
windows were lit by the glow of flat screen TVs
worth twice as much as I've paid in rent a month.
They were doing their job well - keeping the eyes and
Minds off of the reality of the real world around them.

After all, who wants to see a bunch of homeless
people sleeping up and down the sidewalks?
How inconvenient is that?!?? Talk about a buzz kill !
I'd much rather spend my time "unwinding"
with a nice cold beverage - watching a show
that takes my mind off of a long, hard day at work.
Find me something to laugh at,
show me something to keep me entertained;
give me something to capture my attention
and make me feel how I want to feel.
Those people outside - Not my problem.
Let someone else deal with them.
I'm sure they'll find help somewhere.
Besides, there's nothing I can do.
Seriously - what do you expect me to do?!?
(I've got my own problems to worry about)

Guess what? In the time it took to come up with all your excuses
and all the reasons why you couldn't help and what you couldn't
wouldn't shouldn't do - you could have done something.

And whatever thought you just had,
replace it with "Yes, I could have".
Better yet, "Yes, I can and I will."

Because I know that each and every one of us
is capable of doing SOMETHING, no matter
how seemingly small or insignificant.

The biggest lie ever told by anyone -
especially TO YOU and FROM YOU
is that you can't make a difference.

Any time you catch yourself saying
that you're "just this" or "just that"

I hope you smack yourself hard and say
"YOU CAN TAKE YOUR "JUST"
AND JUST SHOVE IT !

Wouldn't it be great to prove yourself wrong
next time you think you can't make a difference?

Oh, by all means - please do !

And while you're at it,
take this to heart and
keep it ever in your head:

" I shall pass this way but once;
  any good, therefore, that I can do
  or any kindness that I can show to
  any human being, let me do it now.
  Let me not defer nor neglect it,
  for I shall not pass this way again. "

The greatest assistance for those in need
does not rest in any program or politician's palm,
but in the hand that is yours –
within reach of another...

Sometimes It Takes A Tragedy

Sometimes it takes a tragedy to cause us
to take hold of our lives and create triumph.

From the rumble of toppled buildings
to crushed & shattered dreams and hopes;
where we go from here all starts at a beginning.

Do we rebuild from rubble with the same anger,
greed, hate and self centered agenda that brought
them down - brought Us down - in the first place?
Are we to hold on forever to those things gone by that
would keep us grounded from taking the steps forward
to a future filled with hope... with peace... with a Love
that leads to real and remaining progress?

Until we move on from the memories that serve to
remind us of our failures - that constantly renew
our fears and tear our hearts as they try and mend;
we will ever remain blind to the beauty and
the blessings that surround us every day.

Yesterday - all of them - are behind us.
Do not live there.
Do not stay there.
Gather from them those things that lift you up
and inspire you to move forward and ahead -
not give you further cause to go back.

Stop pointing at the events passed and
blaming them for where you are,
how you feel and what you do.
The rut you've created by always going back to the past
is making it harder and harder for you to choose
and create a better path for your Life.

Let this day be a turning point from
those things familiar that confine you,
and open your eyes and arms to see and
receive the treasures of today that are here...

Today **IS**
      your day;
Now **is**
      YOUR moment...

Never forget it... and never forget.

dedicated to those lost and the losses of 9-11-2001

What Lead You Here?

What lead you here?

It's a question that often bounces around in my head
when I see someone who has seemingly reached
a rock bottom time in their Life. What happened?

Most people would give you reason after reason
as to why they are where they are - and unwind a
story that would convince at least one of you is true.
Because to them - the storyteller, it is.

The topic came up with a friend as we walked by
what appeared to be a homeless man, and she
shared her own experiences with such people.
"Such people". Sounds like a label - as if they
were any less of a human being than we.
Let's shift that.
You and I, had we made the same decisions and the
same choices they did having been presented the
opportunities and circumstances they experienced -
followed by the actions they took and did not take.
There. Much better.

So, back to our story.
From the most successful among you
to the most down and out - who have
secrets you will take to your grave;
all of you - all of us - have those moments
that we can look back on as pivotal points
as what has made us or broken us in Life.

Yet moments are movements forward -
either toward what we want or what we do not.
One man loses his job, and that is his reason
for standing in the soup line every night.
For another man, he lost his job - and it caused
him to create his own "job", and now he drives
by the very same soup line in his new BMW.
The same circumstance;
One turned it into an opportunity
and a catalyst to succeed -
the other as an excuse.

OK, right about now is when a few may
give me a "Yeah but" speech telling me
about "exceptional" cases and how
so and so's situation is different.
Some may even think some of what
I have, or will more than likely say,
seems to lack a bit of... compassion.

Indeed, it very well could look that way.
It is only that I tend not to coddle for long
ways of thinking, acting, and being that
do not live up to the Miracle that you and I are.

In a World containing
boundless opportunities -
surrounding us with untold resources,
we need never hear nor utter the words;
"THIS happened, so I HAD to do THAT."

Now, you will have good... no, GREAT reason
to do what you do - you always do, always have.
I do. Of course I do! Everything I do is because
I had reason to. It's usually the best reason,
based on what I know and feel at the time.

Events take place and things happen every second.
We act & react to the ones that we are aware of
with the resources and abilities that we know of.

Don't take offense at this - but just keep in mind that
is a very shallow pool   compared to what is available.

All right.
I mentioned to my friend that I'd often wanted to interview
people who seem to have hit rock bottom and find out
how they "got" there. Figuratively for now -
who knows what the future holds.

I know there would be a story,
and whenever some thing or event happened
that the person blamed for their current state,
I'd like to ask them this;

   "When that happened,
   What did you do, and Why?"

See, I'm sure I could hear their excuses and
reasons and come up with a way better plan -
showing them how they could've done this
or that instead and been way better off.
Chances are that you could too!

We are just brilliant and clever like that -
when it comes to other people's problems.
It's when it comes to our own
that we are often shortsighted.

So, enough about people out on the street
who seem so out of reach and out of touch.
Most of us are so absorbed in our own Life
we don't even see the lives around us,
and so consumed by our problems
we can't focus on those of others.

Where are you right now?
What are your reasons for it??

Don't be vague and nebulous with your answers.
Most choices are born of specific circumstances,
often inspired by many - yet it is the "Straw that
broke the camel's back" moment that cinches it.

When that happened,
What did you do, and Why???

Everyone has a reason for doing what they do.

What is yours?

~ **The End** ~
of... ?

There is so much more I'd like to share,
and I hope the opportunity presents itself to do just that.

At the same time, even having read what has been shared,
there is always something more I get out of it each time.
Because just as you have read these, I have numerous times.
And if there wasn't something of great value within the
words, I wouldn't have taken the time to put them here.
Your time is valuable to me.

So I'm going to leave you with a few things
that have made a meaningful difference
in my perspective and how I see things.

>"The results of a given instance
> do not determine the over
> all outcome of the mission."

"Being casual in your Life and about your life
will continue to bring chaos to your doorstep."

>"Be intent in your communication
> with others AND yourself
> be clear in what you say
> and what is and is to be heard..."

"If society as a whole would uplift & encourage the
good & positive that occurs all around us every day
instead of virtually celebrating the sin and storms -
there would be far less to fear in this world...

I'm not saying be naive;
but we gravitate toward that which we see and
hear the most, and whether that is good or bad,
we eventually come to accept and embrace it as "normal"... "

"YOU choose what thoughts
that you allow to simmer and develop
into the actions you will take - and take you -
to where you want to be. Choose wisely."

"Never allow silence to set the tone nor direction
in any endeavor where people are concerned.
For reasons that have always seemed wise at the time,
I have held my tongue when I should have sought
clarity and been silent in my assumptions that
things were or would be "OK".
Consider that it is the highest compliment
for someone to care enough about you to
ask when in doubt and seek clarification
when any matter is not clear.

Seriously - words have so many meanings,
and then we make things up in the silence!
Keep this Kindergarten quote to heart:
"THERE IS NO SUCH THING
AS A STUPID QUESTION !"
If you think you've outgrown that,
you've made an elementary mistake..."

" *The Dash* "

~ Linda Ellis

I read of a man who stood to speak
At the funeral of a friend
He referred to the dates on her tombstone
From the beginning to the end

He noted that first came the date of her birth
And spoke the following date with tears,
But he said what mattered most of all
Was the dash between those years

For that dash represents all the time
That she spent alive on earth.
And now only those who loved her
Know what that little line is worth.

For it matters not how much we own;
The cars, the house, the cash,
What matters is how we live and love
And how we spend our dash.

So think about this long and hard.
Are there things you'd like to change?
For you never know how much time is left,
That can still be rearranged.

If we could just slow down enough
To consider what's true and real
And always try to understand
The way other people feel.

And be less quick to anger,
And show appreciation more
And love the people in our lives
Like we've never loved before.

If we treat each other with respect,
And more often wear a smile
Remembering that this special dash
Might only last a little while.

So, when your eulogy is being read
With your life's actions to rehash
Would you be proud of the things they say
About how you spent your dash? "

> "I have spent my days
> stringing and unstringing my instrument
> while the song I came to sing remains unsung."
> ~Rabindranath Tagore

(What I would add to this is:)
"And waited so long that the Audience,
consumed in silence, dispersed and faded... "

"Do not wait for the perfect thing to do and say,
nor the perfect note to reach or write;
Say it... Sing it... Now. "

The very same sun
that sets on your horizon
is the same for another's sunrise...

All right, now that you are comfortable - regardless
of your level of contentment and circumstance;
Are you ready to stop playing small and step up to the plate?
STOP putting things off and
start pushing yourself to expect
and DEMAND more of yourself
than you are currently accepting.

Throw away the standard you've been following
and allowing to be the regulator and rule of your Life.
YOU start writing the script and playing the lead role;
YOU SET THE STANDARD for what you will receive.
STOP accepting excuses. -
and start reaching for Greatness.

~*Robert H. Steffen*

Made in the USA
Charleston, SC
14 January 2013